VOLUME 1: KS3

Your Rights and Responsibilities

UNDERSTANDING THE ROLE OF THE LAW IN SOCIETY

Edited by Don Rowe and Tony Thorpe

CITIZENSHIP
FOUNDATION

EVANS BROTHERS

Published by Evans Brothers Limited
2A Portman Mansions
Chiltern Street
London W1U 6NR

First published 2002

Some of the material contained in this volume has previously been published
in another form by Hodder and Stoughton

© in the text Citizenship Foundation 2002
© in the watercolour illustrations Evans Brothers Limited 2002

Designed and illustrated by Foundry Design and Production and Rob Chapman
Crabtree Lane, Crabtree Hall, Fulham, London SW6 6TY

Acknowledgements
The publishers would like to thank Rogers, Coleridge and White Ltd for permission to reproduce 'Our
School' from *Salford Road* by Gareth Owen (published by Young Lions, 1988).

British Library Cataloguing in Publication Data
    Rowe, Don, 1946-
        Your Rights and Responsibilities
        Vol. 1
        1. Sociological jurisprudence - juvenile literature
        I. Title
        340.1'15

ISBN 0 237 52310 8

Printed in Hong Kong by Wing King Tong Ltd.

CONTENTS

UNIT 1 NEW CITIZENS
Students
- examine the idea of rights and responsibilities in the context of the community
- understand the link between the values of a group and the nature of the rights and responsibilities of its members who are defined as citizens
- consider the value of education for citizenship

Topic 1: What Now?

Topic 2: Going Anywhere?

UNIT 2 CHILDREN'S RIGHTS
Students
- examine the nature of children's needs
- consider the duties of parents and the state to meet these needs
- understand the position of the child in law
- consider a number of situations relating to the child's position in law

Topic 1: Needs or Rights?

Topic 2: Unfair Treatment?

Topic 3: Growing Up

UNIT 3 DO ANIMALS HAVE RIGHTS?
Students
- examine the legal and moral responsibilities of keeping an animal as a pet
- consider the obligations of pet owners towards both their animals and members of the public
- examine issues surrounding animal rights and how these are publicly debated

Topic 1: For Better and for Worse

Topic 2: Foul!

Topic 3: Out of Control?

Topic 4: Farms not Factories

Topic 5: Campaigning for Change

Topic 6: The Row about Banning Hunting with Dogs

UNIT 4 CAN YOU HEAR ME?
Students
- consider questions of fairness, responsibility and discipline in schools
- examine the purpose of rules, and fair ways of developing and enforcing them
- consider ways in which young people can make their voice heard in school and the community

Topic 1: Appleyard School

Topic 2: That's the Rule

Topic 3: A Better Place

INTRODUCTION

ABOUT THIS SERIES

This series of books for key stages 3 and 4 is based on material developed by the National Curriculum Council's 'Law in Education Project' for key stages 3 and 4. The Law in Education project, which was the precursor of the Citizenship Foundation, was the first national curriculum development project to develop materials for a wide ability range on the rights and responsibilities of citizenship and the role of law in society. This pre-dated the identification of citizenship as a cross-curricular theme of the National Curriculum as introduced in 1989. Prior to that, very few aspects of the law were studied in school beyond topics relating to crime and policing. The former was often encountered in social studies or humanities courses, and the latter sometimes tackled by the school's local police officer. In other words, there was little importance attached to making young people aware of their rights and responsibilities as citizens or helping them understand the nature of democracy and their obligations as voters.

With the introduction of citizenship as a non-statutory cross-curricular theme, the first steps were taken to ensure that all young people were taught something about their legal rights and responsibilities. However, it was not until Curriculum 2000 that this became a statutory entitlement for all pupils. Now, for the first time, all pupils are expected to be taught about their legal rights and duties, how the law works, how it is enforced, and how they can obtain appropriate help and advice. Essentially, this is the kind of knowledge all citizens should have since ignorance of the law is no excuse in a court of law. Indeed, the statement of values, aims and purposes which forms the preface to the new Curriculum, states that one of the principal purposes of education in general is to help young people become 'responsible and caring citizens capable of contributing to the development of a just society'. It should also equip young people to 'make informed judgements and independent decisions and to understand their responsibilities and rights'.

The material developed by the Law in Education Project broke new ground in approaches to teaching and learning about the law, previously thought by many to be too hard for average and less academic pupils. Its success rested on the relevance of the material to young people's lives, the interest generated by study of real cases, and an enquiry-based approach which generated lively debate about a whole range of social justice issues. This new series has drawn on and updated the best and the most relevant of that material and provided additional material to cover elements of the new orders.

WHY 'RIGHTS AND RESPONSIBILITIES'?

It is widely accepted that it is not easy to teach young people about citizenship issues. This is partly because they are still young and relatively uninterested in social affairs or the institutions of the state. However, the present authors have found that young people do want to know about their rights, and that if presented in the right way, teaching about rights naturally raises awareness of the responsibilities that go with them. This kind of approach is best described as 'bottom up', rather than 'top down', because it builds on the experiences and needs of young people themselves. The course is built around the kind of knowledge they need to cope with the complexities of modern life. So, for example, the series covers the main elements of contract law as they relate to buying and selling goods and getting a job and in this way introduces them to the civil law and to an understanding of how it works differently from criminal law.

LAW-RELATED EDUCATION AND 'POLITICAL LITERACY'

The Crick Report, which led up to the introduction of citizenship into Curriculum 2000, recommended that citizenship education should be thought of as having three main strands. These strands describe not the content of citizenship so much as its main aims. The report states that citizenship should promote:

a)   social and moral responsibility
b)   community involvement
c)   political literacy.

These three purposes, if kept in mind during the construction and delivery of citizenship courses, will help to do a number of things. Firstly, they act as a reminder that no amount of legal or civic knowledge is of much use if citizens do not use it with a sense of social responsibility and moral awareness. The development of moral reasoning is something, we argue, that can and should be nurtured throughout the primary years and into the secondary school. For example, while learning about the law, students should be constantly asked to consider why the law is involved in a particular area, what is its purpose, in whose interests the law has been passed, and most importantly, whether it is fair. Students must not be left to think uncritically about the law, as if it is set in stone or always just. It is in the nature of legislation in a democracy that it is constantly under critical review, not only by Parliament, but also by interest groups, the press and the public. In this way, students can be helped to develop a view of Parliament which is not negative, but constructively critical and they will come to see the law as dynamic and relevant to many aspects of their lives. Being politically literate, then, involves more than knowledge of the law, it must include a critical understanding of how to work for change in society and a willingness to get involved.

BECOMING ACTIVE AS CITIZENS

Unlike politics as a theoretical subject, the purpose of citizenship education in schools is a practical one. The phrase often used to describe this is 'being an active citizen'. It is worth reflecting on what is meant by 'active' in this context, because it is often too narrowly interpreted as 'physically doing something of service to others'. In the first place, it is entirely legitimate to take action to assert, defend or even attempt to extend one's own rights. But secondly, it is wrong to underestimate the role of talking in public life as if this is somehow not doing anything. In fact, talk is the principal tool of the citizen. In this sense talk is action and citizenship education has a key role to play in teaching young people how to use the language and ideas of citizenship effectively, how to think critically, reason logically and explain persuasively. There is often an assumption that 'active learning' has to involve activities such as research, role-play, group work and so on. However, we believe that, fundamentally, active learning takes place when, and only when, students genuinely engage with the ideas under consideration. In doing so, they take ownership of the knowledge and bring to bear their own perspectives and experiences as they assimilate these new ideas into their existing conceptual frameworks. This is when knowledge becomes transformed into understanding and is one of the most important stages in the educational process.

DEVELOPING THE SKILLS OF CITIZENSHIP

When using the material in this book, we invite teachers always to be on the lookout to utilize students' existing understandings and experience to engage them in critical analysis. This will certainly involve the development of research skills, but simply retrieving information is not the whole story. Enquiry-based learning only lives up to that name when students adopt the critical stance of the citizen who wants to know 'does this have to be the case?', 'what are the alternatives?', 'what should the law say here?', or 'how could things be improved for the common good?'. Students will eventually come to ask such questions as a habit of mind, but formed through the training of the citizenship class.

The other skills included in the orders are skills of participation and responsible action. Many teachers worry that these phrases have to be understood solely or principally in terms of 'community action', 'community service' or 'volunteering'. Careful reading of the orders suggests that the term 'participation' is first and foremost to be understood in the context of democratic engagement, shared enquiry and in taking responsibility for what goes on in the communal life of the school. Schools are complex communities with many opportunities for students to become engaged, whether this be contributing to the work of the school council, making suggestions for change, becoming peer mediators, running school clubs, helping younger members of the school and so on. Other forms of participative involvement, such as getting involved in local or national campaigns, or practical work in the community flow from this. It must also be borne in mind that not all community service, however worthy it might be, is rich in potential for political learning. Having said this, if students decide to get involved in some form of practical citizenship work, they should always be encouraged to reflect on it and make connections to the work going on in the classroom.

HOW THE MATERIAL IN THIS BOOK IS STRUCTURED

The material in this series covers virtually the whole of the citizenship curriculum without over-rigidly following the bullets in the orders. This is because an approach which draws on real issues and contemporary events cannot easily separate out issues such as rights and responsibilities from matters of justice or government - these matters are often inextricably bound up with each other. We recommend you select from the material in these books to customize a course which best suits the needs and interests of your own students and the constraints of your course planning. Each unit comprises a series of topics on a theme. Teachers' notes for all topics are placed at the beginning of each unit, followed by the copiable pages. Each unit provides a certain amount of information but this is only occasionally given as raw information. Generally the material is presented along with a strategy for learning, which is outlined in the notes. You should feel free to use other methods to present the issues, but should always endeavour to use the material in such as way as to generate the maximum amount of critical analysis and collaborative talk.

ASSESSING WORK IN CITIZENSHIP

The framework for assessing work in citizenship at Key Stage 3 is set down in the attainment target. Students will develop in terms of their own knowledge and understanding and the skills of enquiry, communication, participation and action. Different methods can be used to assess these various elements. Teachers can use the evidence of students' written work to check on the extent to which they have understood the factual elements of the work covered. This might include short pencil and paper tests, responses to newspaper articles, discussion questions and so on. There should not be over-reliance on recall.

Somewhat different is the students' ability to formulate and express their own opinions on social, moral and political issues. Some students operate better orally than in writing, so as the work progresses, it will probably be useful to have a checklist (see below) against which to make a professional judgement for each student over a period of time, not in absolute terms or a national scale but in the context of the form or the year group.

Skills of participation and action might be assessed both in terms of what students demonstrate they can do in class-based group work and in the extent to which they demonstrate responsibility as a member of the form and the year group, as well as interest in and involvement with the wider affairs of the school or the local community. However, it seems wrong to mark down students who have little opportunity to make a positive contribution to the local community, or those whose out-of-school pursuits do not fall into the category of volunteering and yet are developing as perfectly normal and responsible young people.

CHECKLIST FOR ASSESSMENT

Name of student...Form ....

1 = well above average; 2 = above average; 3 = average;
4 = below average; 5 = well below average

Demonstrates knowledge of the factual content of the course 1 2 3 4 5

Shows understanding of key ideas and issues 1 2 3 4 5

Can express and justify a personal opinion in writing......................1 2 3 4 5

Can express and justify a personal opinion orally...........................1 2 3 4 5

Responds appropriately to the opinions of others 1 2 3 4 5

Contributes appropriately to whole class discussions......................1 2 3 4 5

Contributes appropriately to small group discussions......................1 2 3 4 5

Shows interest in social, moral and political issues 1 2 3 4 5

Is able to reflect critcally on experience 1 2 3 4 5

Works co-operatively with others..1 2 3 4 5

Has shown involvement in school and/or community affairs............1 2 3 4 5

UNIT 1

NEW CITIZENS

This unit helps students to

◆ examine the idea of rights and responsibilities in the context of the community;

◆ understand the link between the values of a group and the nature of the rights and responsibilities of its members who are defined as citizens;

◆ consider the value of education for citizenship.

WHAT NOW?

AIMS

◆ To introduce the concepts of rights and responsibilities and explore their links;

◆ To explore the concept of community in relation to rights and responsibilities;

◆ To develop skills of discussion and enquiry around the concepts of fairness.

BACKGROUND

A decision-making game based on the idea of a spaceship crashing onto Mobius, a deserted planet, introduces the concept of rights, responsibilities and community.

This work could easily be spread over a number of lessons according to the time available and the pace and interest of the group.

The Lesson

1. ## A board game

Divide the class into groups of between two and four and explain to students that they are about to play a board game which will give them an introduction to what citizenship is all about. Each group will need a game board, the explanatory sheet which sets the scene and gives instructions and one set of the decision cards (copied and cut up) (see pages 16 to 20). During the game the students are asked to make decisions about situations which tend to place the rights of individuals against their responsibility to the group as a whole. They move more or less quickly according to the decisions they take.

2. ## Class discussion

When students have completed the game, draw things together by asking how quickly the groups made it to the beacon (how many (a) and (b) moves they took) and what kind of group they were according to the panel **WHAT KIND OF GROUP WERE YOU?** (page 17).

● Ask the class to consider the nature of the tensions in many of these situations. Take one or two examples to discuss in more detail. For example, in looking at Decision Card 7, you could ask:

What are the issues here?

- *should individuals have the right to drink from the pond if they please?*
- *what right does the group have to intervene, if any?*
- *at what point would it become justifiable to ban drinking the liquid?*
- *if people wish to drink this liquid what responsibilities should they accept?*
- *what are the parallels with our own society?*

● You could ask each group to say which was the hardest decision they had to reach. Why was it hard? Analyse them together (many students may have considered the issues only superficially during the game). Focus on the tensions between the rights and responsibilities in the situations. Why do they exist? Ask students to think about the fairness of the decisions throughout this discussion.

● Ask students to look again at the decision cards: ask them what different kinds of right are involved in these situations. They could set these out in a grid.

Possible responses include:
- *the right to own property (Decision Cards 6, 16)*
- *the right to be cared for in sickness or old age (2, 5, 9, 11, 12)*
- *the right for children in need to have extra support (4)*
- *the right to be free from anti-social behaviour (1, 8)*
- *the right to inherit property (6)*
- *the right not to be falsely accused of a crime (13)*
- *the right to have a say in matters that affect you (3, 10)*
- *the right to equality of treatment (15)*
- *the right to freedom of choice about your own welfare (7, 12, 14)*
- *the right to justice (13, 16)*

● Ask students why the travellers had responsibilities as well as rights.

Possible responses include:
- *it's a duty to help any fellow human beings in distress or need*
- *you should respect the rights of others if you want them to do this for you*
- *if you belong to a group and want its protection, you should obey its rules*
- *you should always help your friends*

● You could ask students to define the link between rights and responsibilities in general.

Possible responses include:
- *rights cannot be rights if no one respects them*
- *you can lose some rights if you behave badly (eg, the rights to vote and drive)*
- *some rights are not linked to responsibilities and should never be taken away (eg, the right to justice)*

● Ask students whether the travellers had any kind of responsibility to the group as a whole.

Possible responses are:
- *not to slow up progress*
- *to respect majority group decisions*
- *to help defend the group as a whole if necessary*

● Ask students to consider why any of the travellers might not wish to accept the decisions or rules of the whole group.

Possible responses are:
- *they don't like their fellow travellers*
- *they are anti-social*
- *they can't be bothered*
- *they are not able to understand what is going on*
- *they don't care about or respect other people*
- *the decisions or rules might be against their conscience*
- *they might consider the decisions or rules to be unfair or wrong*

● Ask whether any of these reasons are good enough to allow people to opt out of the group or spoil things for others.

● Ask students to consider if any individuals were not prepared to accept these responsibilities, whether it would be acceptable for the group as a whole to impose them through, for example, punishments. What would make it acceptable?

Possible responses include:
- *the 'greater good': if lives will be saved*
- *the majority knows best and can do what it likes*
- *sometimes people have to be taught how to be 'good citizens'*

● Now ask students to think about what would be the fairest way for the group to make decisions (see cards 3 and 10).

Possible responses include:
- *appoint a leader to take decisions quickly*
- *let the strongest leader emerge*
- *elect a committee of leaders*
- *have no leaders (anarchy) and decide everything democratically*
- *decide on major issues democratically and delegate others to committees*

● As a conclusion to this section of the lesson, ask students to consider what makes a decision a fair one.

Possible responses include:
- *if it's made by a democratically elected group*
- *if the result is fair between the parties involved*
- *if it conforms strictly to an established rule*
- *if it agrees with your personal conscience*

3. **Drawing conclusions**

Point out that any group of people which has to work together needs to develop settled ways of working. The group then becomes a community. A community is not just a random collection of people, **its members have some aims in common and have developed some common values and ways of working together.**

● Tell students that, when the Mobius survivors decided to stick together and not go it alone, they became a community, which they were not when they were just travelling along together before the disaster. Ask what were the aims of the whole community of survivors on Mobius?

Possible responses include:
- *for as many to survive as possible*
- *to help each other out when in need (mutual support)*
- *to provide human comfort, company and encouragement*
- *to protect the weaker members from those who would abuse them*
- *to use the resources of the whole group to achieve survival*

● We all belong to different communities. Ask students which ones they can think of and then to consider in what ways these are communities more than just random collections of individuals (like people in a shop or on a beach).

● People often live together in a street, town or city. Ask students to consider whether that makes them into a community and what it is about families, schools, neighbourhoods and countries that makes them communities (i.e. what do the people in these groups have in common and what are the aims of the communities?)

● Some communities are made up of people we love or are very close to. Other communities have people in them that we do not like or have much in common with. Ask students to consider what the difference between these two groups is in terms of how we get along with them.

Possible responses include:
- *we relate to our friends and relations on the basis of affection, knowing them well, wanting their friendship and not wishing to hurt them*
- *we have to relate to people we do not like or know well on the basis of respect for their rights and mutual cooperation*

● Discuss in what ways it could be said that the whole world is a community.

Possible responses are:
- *it's made up of fellow human beings, whatever their race, creed, etc*
- *human survival depends on global cooperation*
- *humanity and the animal kingdom have much in common and depend on each other*
- *good people around the world should work together to fight illness, poverty, crime, abuse of human rights*

● Ask students to consider whether all decent communities are democracies.

Possible responses include
- *not necessarily, what about families and schools?*
- *no, but even communities which are not democratic can consult members*

4.   **A link to the next topic**

Explain to students that, when communities come into existence, they need common ways of working. Some of this will be influenced by the reason the group has come together. For example, on Mobius the survivors needed to get to the beacon as quickly as possible and that affected the way they made their decisions. But it could be different if they knew they were going to be there for a long time. Tell students that this is the focus of the next topic.

TOPIC TWO

GOING ANYWHERE?

AIMS

◆ **To introduce the concept of 'citizens' and 'citizenship' within the context of community;**

◆ **To explore the idea that rights and responsibilities can differ between communities;**

◆ **To demonstrate the importance of asking whether social rules and practices are fair;**

◆ **To consider the value of education for citizenship.**

BACKGROUND

When the space travellers realise they are marooned on Mobius they have to establish the beginnings of a settled community, which raises questions about the best way to run things. This means they have to work out some basic principles of government. Unfortunately they do not all agree on what is best.

THE LESSON

1.   The board game revisited

Remind students of their difficult journey to the beacon on Mobius. Tell them that, unfortunately, when the travellers arrived they found that the beacon itself had been damaged and they were unable to communicate with Earth. Now they are stuck on Mobius and have no idea how long they might be there. There are over 50 survivors including a dozen or so children and a few elderly people. The group is fairly mixed in terms of race and religion.

They are going to have to set up a community on the planet and hope that one day they will be rescued. Explain that, for a few weeks, things go reasonably smoothly. Everyone helps each other in building shelters and gathering food.

However, it is not too long before murmurs of unrest start to be heard. It is becoming clearer as each day goes by that the large group of survivors needs proper leadership to run things in a more organised way and make careful plans for the future.

Unfortunately, people disagree over how decisions like this should be taken. Some survivors, (democrats, nicknamed 'Demos'), believe the group should be as democratic as possible. Decisions should be taken by everyone involved. Others, (autocrats, nicknamed 'Autos'), seem to prefer a small group of people to lead the group under one strong leader.

2.   Role play

Role-play a public meeting to try to decide which type of leadership will be best for the group. Encourage students to explore the advantages and disadvantages of each type of leadership. The class could be divided in half to role-play different positions. Prepare the arguments first in pairs or small groups. Elect someone from the class to chair the meeting. Before you begin ask students what rules they will need to establish to make sure everyone gets a fair hearing. Point out that some people have very good ideas but find it hard to speak out in large groups. Ask if there is a way of helping them to express their opinions.

Secretly prime some of the 'Autos' not to accept a vote at the end of the meeting. Follow up the effects of this refusal later in the lesson (see point 5 on page 14).

3.   **Class discussion**

Debrief the public meeting. Discuss the advantages and disadvantages of both positions.

Possible points to cover include:

Democrats
  - *everyone has a chance to have their say*
  - *the views of minorities will be listened to*
  - *decisions are likely to be fairer to all members*
  - *people will accept group decisions better if they have had a say*
  - *working this way sends out a signal that everyone is valued*

BUT
  - *there is hardly the time to discuss everything democratically*
  - *sometimes the best ideas are not shared by the majority of people*
  - *sometimes problems are too complicated to be discussed by everyone*
  - *it is possible for democratic decisions to be unfair to minority groups*
  - *people don't always abide by the majority if they feel strongly*
       about something

Autocrats
  - *decisions can be made by those with real qualities of leadership*
  - *not everyone wants to be bothered with community affairs*
  - *lots of problems are too hard for ordinary group members to understand*
  - *a group full of people with different ideas needs to be told what to do*
  - *having one strong leader saves time in decision making*
  - *strong leadership cuts out all the whingeing and negative comments*
       people often make if they expect to have their way

BUT
  - *autocrats might make decisions in their own interests and not the group's*
  - *minority groups might become ignored or discontented*
  - *people need to feel they belong, or 'have a stake', in their community*
  - *people's basic rights could be ignored by a single strong leader*
  - *it could be difficult to stop the community becoming unfair and unequal*
  - *it will be difficult for people to protest against the leadership*

4.   **Written work**

Some of these pros and cons might be written up in a grid or as a discussion question.

5.   **Group work**

Recap by reminding students that no agreement was reached at the end of the public meeting. The autocrats refused to vote and the meeting ended in chaos! Unfortunately, the community now splits into two factions who go their separate ways, living in different areas of Mobius. So there are two communities on Mobius each running things in a different way. Tell students that they will be allocated to the 'Demos' or 'Autos' to consider one or two new problems. Read **YOU DECIDE** (page 21) and ask students in the groups to which they have been allocated to consider the questions on the page.

6.   **Class discussion**

Discuss and compare the answers of the two main groups. What kind of differences have the students come up with? Is there any room for compromise between the two groups?

Discuss which of these two communities the students would prefer to belong to, and why.

7.   **Drawing conclusions**

Tell students that what they have been through in this exercise, is a little like what happens when new countries or states are born and new ways of working have to be developed. The 'Autos' and 'Demos' are really citizens of tiny states. The citizens of a state are people who belong to that community. Citizens of a country have the rights and responsibilities which their laws give them.

Tell students that on Mobius they were asked to think about the best way to make the rules. There is a difference between the actual rules (laws) of a society and the rules about how they are made (this is called the constitution). If there is a school council, it will have a constitution. If students are members of a society, it will also have a constitution.

Ask students how important they think it is for people to understand the constitutions of the societies they belong to.

Possible responses include:
- *so that people know what they can and can't do*
- *so that people know who has power*
- *so that people know how to change things*
- *so that people who abuse their power or responsibilities can be stopped*

Ask how important it is for societies to have rules and constitutions which are fair.

Possible responses include:
- *it is just right*
- *because otherwise minority groups will get overlooked or worse*
- *because people might not put up with living in a society that's unfair*

BUT
- *people do not agree on what is fair*
- *fairness might be seen as allowing everyone just to look out for themselves*
- *fairness might be seen as asking people to care for the less fortunate*

7.   **Written work**

Students could write a short story about the 'Autos' on Mobius who decide that they want to change the way their society is run, or a story set in a school or a youth club in which the members decide they want more of a say in their own affairs.

8.   **Class discussion**

Ask how important they think it is for schools to have compulsory citizenship education.

Possible responses include:

Important
- *people should know what rights they have and how to claim them*
- *people should know what responsibilities they have and be given the skills to carry them out*
- *people should know the law and how it works*
- *people should be able to decide whether laws are fair and how to try to get them changed if they are not*
- *people should know what kind of society they want and who to vote for*
- *people should be able to see if something needs doing and to take action, because the law will not always make sure that people get everything they need or deserve*

Not important
- *it's too complicated for ordinary people to understand*
- *it's not for kids, we should wait until we're grown up*
- *it's too boring*

It would be useful to tell students at this point that this unit has been an introduction to the others in the series, in which they will take a closer look at their rights and responsibilities, examine what it means to be a citizen and come to understand more about how society works and how it might be made better. In this way, it is hoped that when they come to vote, they will have a much better idea of how to make the law work for them and how to use their vote in the way which will help make the kind of society they want to live in.

WHAT NOW?

DREAM HOLIDAY TURNS TO NIGHTMARE

The Cosmic Holiday's spacecruiser "Voyager" on the way from Earth to the holiday planet of Funfaria has run into a meteorite storm. The craft has been severely damaged and all communications systems are destroyed before a distress signal can be sent. The pilot has managed to crash-land upon Mobius, the nearest planet.

The planet is almost unexplored but the survivors of the crashed ship know that it has an oxygen atmosphere similar to that of Earth and that past travellers installed a rescue beacon at Mobius's northern pole. Unfortunately, the spacecraft has crashed near the opposite pole. The journey to the beacon could take months.

You are amongst the large group of survivors who are beginning the journey to the beacon. You have managed to salvage some food and supplies but, as you travel, a number of situations arise which together you have to tackle. If problems are not sorted out speedily, the whole group may suffer and you may never make it to the beacon.

☆☆ ☆ HOW TO PLAY THE GAME

1 Arrange yourselves in groups of about four.

2 You will be given a board, on which you record your progress, and 16 cards.

3 Shuffle the cards and place them face down in a pile.

4 In turns, read out the problems you have to overcome. On each decision card, your group must decide between two choices **A** or **B** according to what you agree is right. Try to reach an agreement without voting, if you can.

5 After the first decision is made, shade in your progress sheet. If you decide on **A**, shade in one section. If you decide on **B** shade in two sections. (Use different colours to record **A** and **B** decisions.)

6 Now read the next decision card, make your decision and shade in one **A** or two **B** sections. Although **B** choices score higher than **A**, you must not choose **B** answers just to get on quickly. Always do what the group thinks is right, no matter how slowly this means you travel.

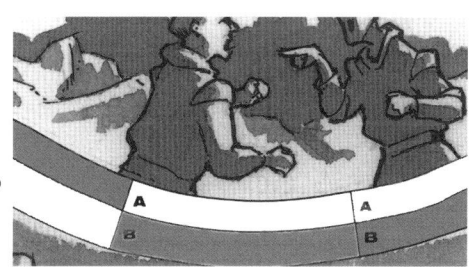

7 You don't have to finish on the exact number of sections. Your final decision may be an **A** decision or a **B** decision.

8 When you get to the beacon (well done, your group has survived) count the number of moves you made (both **A** and **B** decisions count as one move). Look at the chart below to find out what kind of group you were. Then divide your moves into **A** and **B** scores and enter each total in the box at the bottom of the board. Look closely at how many times you decided in favour of the individual rather than the group.

9 Compare the speed of your progress with that of other groups.

WHAT KIND OF GROUP WERE YOU?

8-10 moves	Your decisions have helped the whole party quickly reach the beacon but some people might have been lost on the way.
11-13 moves	You have tried to move the group on as quickly as possible but you haven't ignored the needs of certain members of the group.
14-16 moves	You have put the wishes of the individual members of the party before the needs of the whole group. This has meant that the journey has taken longer.

DECISION CARD 1

One member of the party enjoys singing. Unfortunately, she sings all the time. Some people don't mind but a few say it's driving them mad. Do you:
A)   Do nothing and allow her to sing whenever she wants to?
B)   Demand that she stops singing when others are about?

DECISION CARD 2

A few people who were injured in the landing are slowing things down. You fear that at your present rate of progress you may not make it to the beacon before your food runs out. Do you:
A)   Slow down to their pace and risk the lives of everyone?
B)   Leave them, possibly to die?

DECISION CARD 3

There are disagreements about who should lead the party. Giving everyone a chance to have a say is wasting a lot of time. Do you:
A)   Keep the system in which everyone has a chance to voice her or his opinion?
B)   Vote for one leader who can take decisions quickly?

DECISION CARD 4

Members of one family with a badly handicapped child claim that they can't look after her properly. The child is suffering. Do you:
A)   Provide the family with an extra person to help them cope?
B)   Do nothing. Leave the family to sort out its own problem?

DECISION CARD 5

A baby is born to one of the party. The baby is ill, and will probably die if moved. Do you:
A)   Hold up the party until mother and child can travel?
B)   Carry on and hope that the baby survives?

DECISION CARD 6

An old lady dies. It is discovered that she was carrying a large amount of money which her daughter claims is now hers. Do you:
A)   Allow the daughter to keep the money?
B)   Make her hand the money in, so she can't use it to buy unfair amounts of rations?

DECISION CARD 7

The group comes across a pond containing a pale green liquid. The liquid has the effect of cheering people up, but some people are drinking too much which makes them lazy. Do you:
A)   Allow them to drink it?
B)   Ban all drinking of the pond water?

DECISION CARD 8

A 14-year-old is behaving very badly, disrupting the progress of the group. His parents can't control him but refuse to let anyone else try. Do you:
A)   Respect the parents' wishes?
B)   Put the child with another family?

DECISION CARD 9

One of the leaders of the party has been taken ill and needs a blood transfusion. Several people have the same blood group but no one wants to volunteer, for fear of infection. Do you:
A) Allow people to refuse if they want to?
B) Force people to give blood if necessary?

DECISION CARD 10

One person is always criticising the way the group is being led. His comments are affecting the attitudes of others. Do you:
A) Allow him to continue?
B) Tell him to keep quiet and separate him from the others?

DECISION CARD 11

One member of the group is refusing to carry out the tasks given to her. She says there is no point - they are all doomed. She is very depressed. Do you:
A) Leave her alone and let her do what she wants?
B) Threaten to punish her if she doesn't work?

DECISION CARD 12

An elderly couple, who feel they are holding the group back, volunteer to be left behind. Do you:
A) Help them to cope with the journey?
B) Accept the offer?

DECISION CARD 13

You discover that the person you have put in charge of the food stores has spent six years in prison for theft. Until now he has been doing a very good job. Do you:
A) Trust him and let him carry on with the work?
B) Take no chances and put someone else in charge of the food?

DECISION CARD 14

There's a feud going on between two of the survivors. They plan to settle it with a fight tonight. Do you:
A) Let them get on with it?
B) Stop the fight in case others are tempted to join in?

DECISION CARD 15

The weather on the planet is very cold. Some of the passengers lost their warm clothing when the spaceship crashed. Do you:
A) Allow people to keep their own clothes, as sooner or later things will start to wear out?
B) Make everyone share out clothing equally?

DECISION CARD 16

There has been an outbreak of stealing. A woman is caught taking money from a handbag. Do you:
A) Punish her for the one crime you know she has committed?
B) Punish her very severely to make an example of her?

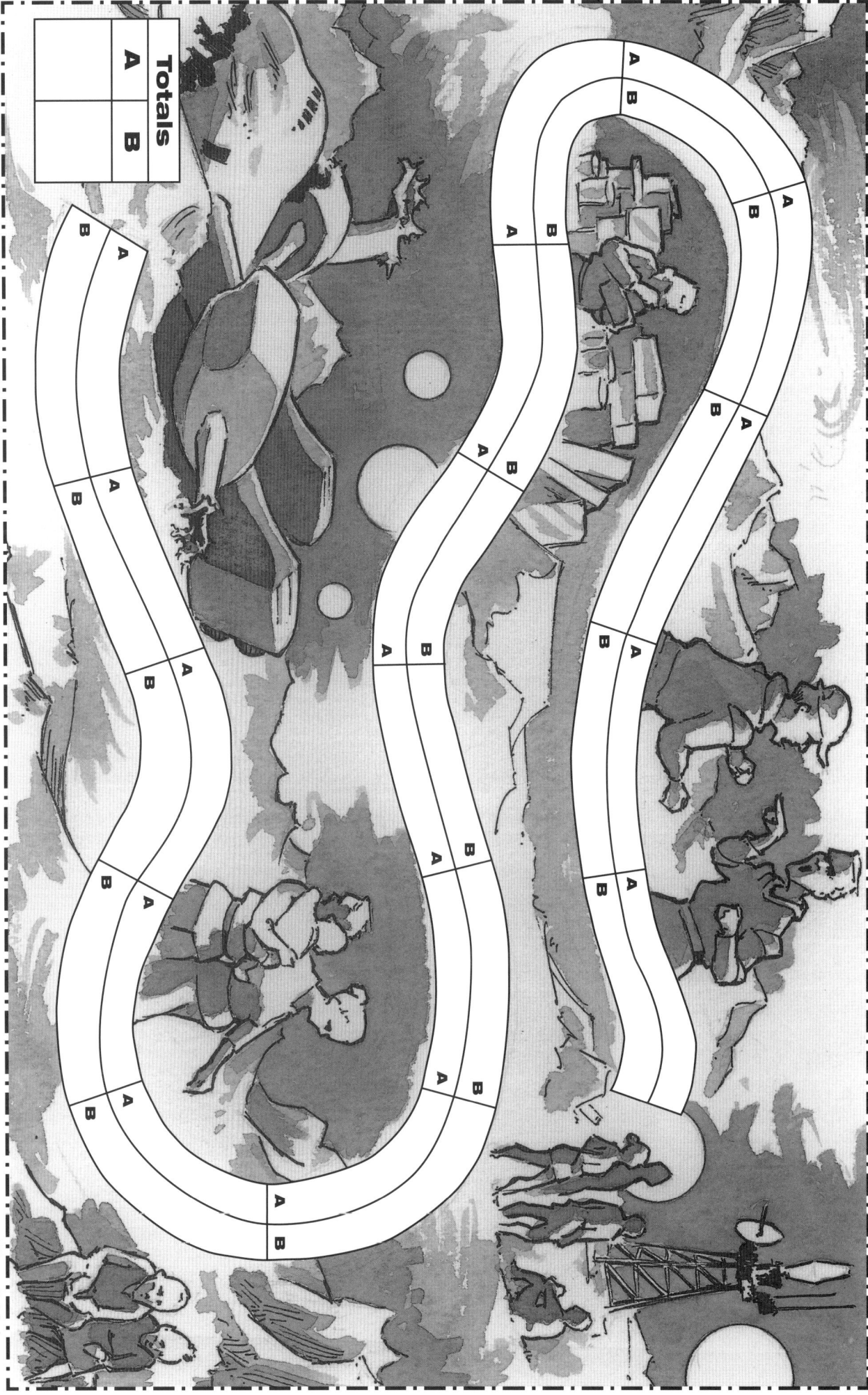

Totals	
A	**B**

GOING ANYWHERE?

You Decide

DEMOCRATS

'Demos' believe that decisions should be as far as possible taken by everyone. Smaller committees could be set up to carry out tasks set by the whole group.

AUTOCRATS

'Autos' believe that one leader with a small group of supporters should take command. The leader decides everything and the group of 'ministers' takes control of areas like food supply, buildings, transport, family affairs and 'security'.

You are either a 'Demo' or an 'Auto'. In small groups of 'Demos' or 'Autos', think about the following issues you will face on Mobius in the coming months:

1 What will you do when someone breaks the rules of your community? Think of the best way to deal with offenders and carry out justice.

2 What will you do when someone from the other group wishes to leave them and join you? Will you force any conditions on them?

3 How will you decide how to share out property, food and welfare in your group?

4 What will you do when a small minority group asks permission to observe a Holy Day (which means not doing any work on that day). They say it offends them when others work on that day.

5 What should your group do about someone who is beginning to complain about the way some of the decisions have recently been taken?

6 Decide whether you will need a code of basic rights (eg, the right to a trial if accused of a crime) which can apply to all members of your community. Then make some suggestions about what rights everyone in your group should have.

If possible, share your ideas with your fellow 'Demos' or 'Autos'.

UNIT 2

CHILDREN'S RIGHTS

This unit helps students to

◆ examine the nature of children's needs;

◆ consider the duties of parents and the state to meet these needs;

◆ understand the position of the child in law;

◆ consider a number of situations relating to the child's position in law.

TOPIC ONE

NEEDS OR RIGHTS?

AIM

◆ To introduce the concept of children's rights and consider who is responsible for their provision.

BACKGROUND

A story of an abandoned baby is used to focus attention on children's basic rights, before introducing students to the United Nations Convention on the Rights of the Child, which came into force in September 1990.

The 54 articles making up the Convention outline the nature of governments' and parents' responsibilities with regard to child welfare. There are two ways in which UN member countries may support the Convention. The first is by signing it. This is of symbolic importance and indicates a nation's willingness to give serious consideration to the document. More than 130 countries have taken this step, including the United Kingdom. The second way in which the Convention is acted upon is known as ratification and indicates a state's intention to incorporate the Convention into its own body of law.

After two years of hesitation the UK government finally ratified the Convention in December 1991, whilst reserving the right to opt out over certain issues including immigration, the employment of 16- to 18-year-olds and the locking up of some young offenders in adult prisons where this was necessary because of a lack of more suitable accommodation. Whilst this may seem disappointing to some, it should be noted that the UK has a better than average record of abiding by the international charters it has ratified. Some countries have allowed gross breaches of their articles to continue after signing these documents.

THE LESSON

1. **A newspaper story**

Ask the students to read the newspaper story **TWO DAY OLD BABY ABANDONED** (page 29).

2. **Small groups**

In groups of twos or threes, ask the students to list the immediate needs of the little girl who has been found and to consider how and by whom these needs should be met.

3. **Class discussion**

Gather ideas from the whole class, inviting each group to contribute one item in turn, until all ideas have been exhausted.

4. **Small groups**

Now ask the students to think about the little girl's basic needs when she is older – perhaps their age. Will these needs have changed? What will they be and how should they be met?

5. **Written work**

Conclude this section of the lesson by asking students to draw up a complete list of their ideas of children's basic needs. This could be presented in the form of a charter entitled All children need... . Some students may wish to present this in the style of an old document (in which case, the activity may be more appropriate as a homework exercise).

6. **A Children's Charter**

Tell the students that many of the basic human needs that they have listed in the first part of the topic are today seen as something which everybody should have and are known as rights. Explain that the Convention on the Rights of the Child, written under the auspices of the United Nations, is an attempt to obtain support for these rights from all countries, and a commitment to provide for them within their constitutions. Ask students to read A CHILDREN'S CHARTER (page 30).

7. **Small groups**

Ask groups to compare their lists of basic needs with the (simplified) charter and to comment on similarities and differences.

8 **Class discussion**

Ask students to choose just two rights from the Convention. This can be approached in a number of ways, including a balloon exercise, where students imagine they have to jettison rights, two at a time, in order to stay airborne. The last two rights they retain are those they hold to be the most important rights of all.

9. **An extension activity**

You could ask students to choose just one of the rights listed in the Convention to discover how this right is observed in this country or elsewhere. Ask them to find out how it is being broken and what is being done to prevent this happening. Two cases are offered (on pages 31 and 32) as examples, one from this country and one from overseas.
See the section RESOURCES (page 28) for a list of useful websites to help students with their research.

TOPIC TWO

UNFAIR TREATMENT?

AIM

> To show that in England and Wales the law requires courts to consider the welfare of a child to be of paramount importance and to enable students to apply this to a practical example.

NOTE

This topic raises sensitive issues which may have a close bearing on the lives of some pupils. It is important to read the materials carefully before using them in the classroom in order to assess their likely impact on individual pupils. This topic should not be undertaken if its effects are likely to be detrimental to any pupils in the group.

Guidance on the procedures to be followed by teachers where cases of neglect or abuse of children are suspected is available from senior staff in all schools. Concern over a pupil should be communicated immediately to the head teacher or a senior member of staff.

BACKGROUND

Using the case study of a boy who was badly mistreated by his parents, pupils consider the laws protecting children from abuse.

Parents have a legal duty to maintain and protect their children and ensure they are not ill-treated or exposed to physical or moral danger. However, there are no laws in England and Wales which specify the precise responsibilities and duties of parenthood. In the 1988 Law Commission Report on Guardianship and Custody it is argued that it is not practicable in law to list those factors that comprise parental responsibility, as such a list would have to change from time to time to meet differing needs and circumstances.

The law, however, does indicate when a parent may fail in his or her duty towards a child. In the **Children and Young Persons Act 1933**, it states that it is an offence for any person over the age of 16 who has the custody, charge or care of a child to assault, ill-treat, neglect, abandon or expose that child or young person to any danger. Neglect is taken in the Act to include the failure to provide adequate food, clothing, medical aid or lodging.

The **Children Act 1989** sets out the procedure which courts and officials are required to follow in dealing with cases involving the neglect and abuse of children. The law states that the welfare of the child is of paramount importance. It requires speedy and effective action from the authorities, but underlines the need to balance the rights of the parent with the general duty of every authority to safeguard the welfare of the child. At the end of this topic, it is important that pupils are not left with the impression that the law discriminates against parents nor with a fear of disclosing a concern to somebody who may be able to offer help.

THE LESSON

1.   **A story**

Read the story of **THE BOY WHOSE BEDROOM WAS A CELL** (page 33) with the class. Explain that it is based on a real-life case, and that the names have been changed. Invite students' initial reactions including what they think Chris can do and what difficulties face him in deciding on a course of action. Then move on to look in more detail at **WHAT THE LAW SAYS** (page 34), which gives a summary of the law dealing with the neglect of children. What things which have happened to Chris are against the law? Compare also with the UN Convention on the Rights of the Child. Read **TAKING ACTION** (page 34) which describes how Chris discloses his situation to his form tutor, who informs the head teacher of the school. Ask students what they think would be the best thing to do for Chris.

2.   **Class discussion**

Keeping the discussion at a general level, encourage students to recognise the seriousness and difficulty of such cases and the dilemmas which authorities face in dealing with them.

Ask students to discuss what is in the best interests of Chris's brothers and sisters and whether Chris's mother and stepfather should be punished for the way in which he had been treated.

Tell students that, in the case upon which this story is based, Chris was placed in the care of the local authority. His mother was charged with neglect and assault, found guilty and sent to prison. Chris's stepfather was not charged and retained responsibility for the other members of the family. Ask the class to consider why they think the mother might have been punished more severely than Chris's stepfather, and if they think this was fair.

TOPIC THREE

GROWING UP

AIM

◆   **To consider some issues of conflict between parents and their children as the children grow towards independence.**

BACKGROUND

In law, parental responsibility does not wholly disappear until a young person reaches the age of 18. Parents' rights are dwindling rights which the courts will hesitate to enforce against a child, and the more so the older she or he is. As Lord Denning stated in a case in 1969, 'parental power starts with the right of control and ends with little more than advice'.

THE LESSON

1.   Introduction

Introduce this topic by explaining that in some areas of law there are clearly defined points marking the shift from childhood to adult responsibilities. Ask students to read the sheets on YOUR LEGAL RIGHTS (pages 35 to 38).

2.   Class discussion

Discuss which of these age laws are regarded as unfair by some people. For example, some argue that voting rights should be allowed to 16-year-olds, since many young people begin to pay taxes at this age.

3.   Small groups

Explain that many of the changes in a young person's life are not marked in a clearly defined way. Ask students to look at the cartoons under the heading RIGHT OR WRONG? (page 39). Talk about what is happening in each one and then ask them to discuss, in their groups, whether each person should have what she or he is asking for, and if so, how the parent might be won over or persuaded. What good arguments might parents offer in support of their case?

4.   Role play

If time allows, ask students to select one of the cases and prepare a piece of writing or drama around the point at which the parent is asked by the young person to change his or her mind.

Encourage students, before beginning their story or play, to decide what they want their work to show. There are a range of themes which can be developed from such situations, including those of concern, control (parents), frustration and individuality (the child). Place a time limit on each piece of drama and ensure that enough time is left at the end of the lesson for at least some groups to share their work with the rest of the class. Allow the class to respond to how some of these issues were handled.

RESOURCES

Further information on the United Nations Convention on the Rights of the Child is available from the United Nations Information Centre, Millbank Tower, 21–24 Millbank, London SW1P 4QH. 020 7630 1981.

Guidance on the procedures to be followed by teachers when it is suspected that a pupil may be a victim of abuse or neglect is available for senior staff in all schools. Advice is also published by teachers' unions and associations.

Work on this unit may raise questions from pupils requiring specialist answers. This is obtainable from the NSPCC, 42 Curtain Rd, London EC2A 3NH. 020 7825 2500. The NSPCC also operates a free national helpline on child protection issues for both adults and children on 0808 800 5000.

Kidscape, 2 Grosvenor Gdns, London SW1W ODH, 020 7730 3300 is able to provide general advice for children, parents and teachers on bullying and keeping children safe. A list of publications is available on receipt of a stamped addressed envelope.

The Children's Legal Centre monitors all aspects of the law as it affects children' rights. It advises government on policy and offers advice to young people and those who work with them. Their advice line is 01206 873820 or they can be contacted at www2.essex ac.uk/clc.

Childline is a free national helpline for children and young people in trouble with any problem. It provides a confidential telephone counselling service 24 hours a day. Young people can write to Childline, FREEPOST 1111, London Nl OBR or telephone 0800 1111.

USEFUL WEBSITES

www.howardleague.org
www.unicef.org.uk
www.traidcraft.co.uk
www.bbc.co.uk
www.europe.cnn.com
www.nspcc.org.uk
www.kidscape.org.uk
www.unitednations.org.uk

NEEDS OR RIGHTS?

THE DAILY HERALD

TWO DAY OLD BABY ABANDONED!

THE CRIES of a two day old baby attracted the attention of a cleaner at Victoria Station in the early hours of yesterday morning. The baby, a girl, dressed in warm clothes, was lying in a cardboard box outside the entrance to the station.

Written on an envelope placed inside the box was the message 'Please look after me'. The police have made an appeal for the girl's parents to come forward and have contacted hospitals and doctors' surgeries in the area.

The baby girl is being cared for at St Thomas's Hospital. Nurses have named her Victoria, after the station at which she was found.

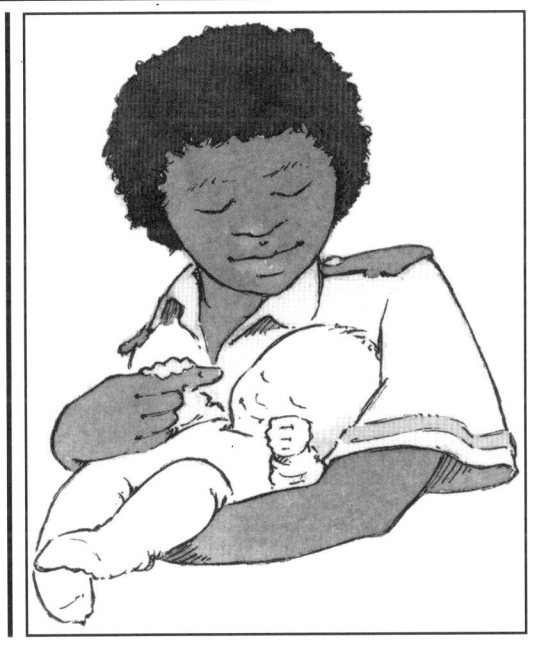

EVERY CHILD SHOULD HAVE ONE

This little girl has not had a very good start in life. In cases like this the police can sometimes find the baby's mother or father, but usually someone must be found to look after the child.

☆ Make a list of all the little girl's basic needs.
☆ How should they be met?

As she gets older, the girl's needs will change.

☆ What will be her basic needs when she is your age?
☆ How should they be met?

A CHILDREN'S CHARTER

In 1990 most of the countries in the world signed an agreement which set out the ways in which all children should be treated, no matter where they come from or who they are. This agreement is called The United Nations Convention on the Rights of the Child.

A right is something which people think everyone should have.

Here is a list of the main points in the 1990 United Nations Convention on the Rights of the Child. A child here means every person under the age of 18.

❶ **All children should be treated equally. A child's or its parent's sex, colour, language, religion or disability should not affect this in any way.**

❷ **When dealing with children, official groups such as the police, doctors, schools and the courts should act in what they think are the best interests of the child.**

❸ **Every child has a right to life, and everything should be done by the government to make sure a child grows up in healthy surroundings.**

❹ **All children should have a name, a nationality and the right to know and be looked after by his or her parents.**

❺ **A child has the right to express an opinion freely and for that opinion to be taken into account by those dealing with the child.**

❻ **Children should be free to choose their religion and friends, as long as this does not in some way damage the rights and freedoms of others.**

❼ **No child should be treated or punished in a cruel or inhuman way, or be deprived of liberty.**

❽ **Disabled children shall have the right to special care to help them enjoy as full a life as possible.**

❾ **All children should have a standard of living which helps them fully develop. It is the job of the parents to provide this – but if it cannot be done, the state should make sure this is being done.**

❿ **Children should have a free education which helps them develop to the full.**

⓫ **No child should carry out work which is harmful or interferes with her or his education.**

⓬ **No child under the age of 15 should be allowed to join the armed forces.**

THE CAMPAIGN FOR
CHILDREN'S RIGHTS:
CASE STUDY 1

Should children go to prison?

Children are still being held in prison in unsuitable conditions for young people, according to campaigners. The Howard League for Penal Reform has been collecting evidence on this practice stretching back 20 years.

For example at the Portland Young Offender Institute, where boys as young as 15 have been held, they found evidence of physical and mental cruelty by members of staff towards inmates. Boys have been kicked, punched and had their heads smashed against brick walls.

On receiving this evidence from the Howard League, the prison governor suspended four officers and called in the police. The government decided that Portland was no longer suitable for young people under 18.

At another Young Offender Institution, holding 15-21-year-olds, the Chief Inspector of Prisons found that the younger boys were in great fear of being bullied by the older ones. There was also a terrible level of neglect and lack of understanding on the part of those who ran the prison, the Inspector said. There were three suicides at the prison in 2000 and many cases of young prisoners harming themselves – a sign of distress and mental ill health.

The Howard League claimed that locking up children in this way failed to help them, and did not prevent them from offending again once they were released.

31

THE CAMPAIGN FOR CHILDREN'S RIGHTS:
CASE STUDY 2

Child slavery in Africa

Although the slave trade was banned in Africa as long ago as the 1880s, many children of poor families are still being sold by parents to traders for as little as US$1.50. Surpisingly, perhaps, more girls than boys are sold into slavery. One reason for this is that many parents cannot afford the cost of their daughters' weddings. Traders may also prefer girls because they are less rebellious as they grow older. Girls often work as servants for the rich or in the markets, whilst boys are set to work in cotton and cocoa plantations. Cocoa is the main ingredient in chocolate.

International charities, such as UNICEF and Anti-slavery International, have known about this problem for a long time. They say slavery in parts of West and Central Africa never died out. The problem is really that the families are extremely poor, say the charities. Traders look out for large families with too many children for the parents to support. Some parents are unaware of what is really happening. They are led to believe that that the children are going off to a better life and education.

But things can get better. British chocolate makers are coming under greater public pressure to make sure that they do not buy supplies from plantations where there are child slaves. And the Fairtrade movement is growing in strength. People buy Fairtrade products knowing that conditions under which these products are made have been carefully checked.

UNFAIR TREATMENT?

THE BOY WHOSE BEDROOM WAS A CELL

Chris is eleven and he has four brothers and sisters of whom he is very fond. He is the eldest in the family, but for some reason his mum and stepfather treat him differently from the others. Chris sleeps and lives by himself. When he gets home from school his mother sends him to his room in the attic where he has a meal and stays for the rest of the night.

Chris spends his time alone. He does not see or talk to anybody. He can't wave to his friends because the window in his room is boarded up. He has just a small table and chair, a bed, a sleeping bag and a pot for a toilet. He has a light to do his homework, but when he has finished, the bulb is taken out and he is left in darkness. His stepfather never comes up to see him, and if Chris complains to his mother, she hits him.

Chris is treated like this every day of the year. Even on his birthday and at Christmas he stays alone - and always without any presents.

WHAT THE LAW SAYS

In England and Wales the law says that ...

It is an offence for anyone aged 16 and over and in charge of a child to purposely ill treat, abandon or put that child in any danger.

It is an offence for a parent to neglect a child and endanger that child's health by not providing enough food, clothing or medical help.

TAKING ACTION

One morning Mr Marshall, Chris's form tutor, asked him about a bruise on his face. Chris said nothing at first, but went back to Mr Marshall at lunchtime and told him all about his life at home.

Mr Marshall told Chris that he would have to tell the head of the school what Chris had said and that she would immediately be getting in touch with Social Services.

Something had to be done quickly for Chris.

The law says that in cases like this, the interests and good of the child must be put before everything else.

GROWING UP
YOUR LEGAL RIGHTS

Until you are 21, you cannot gain your full legal rights. But the freedoms and responsibilities of adulthood do not all come at one moment - they are gained over a period of several years. The following information provides a short guide to your legal rights from the time you are a baby to the age of 21.

A baby can

- ✔ own and inherit money and goods.
- ✔ have a savings account at a building society, bank or Post Office, but its parents sign the papers.
- ✔ hold a full passport.

From the age of 5 a child

- ✔ must receive full-time education. The responsibility for this lies both with the parents and with local education authority.
- ✔ may be given alcohol, except in the bar of a public house.

From the age of 7 a child

- ✔ is allowed to sign and draw money from his or her bank, Post Office and building society savings account.

From the age of 10 a child

- ✔ can be convicted of criminal offences.

From the age of 12 a young person

- ✔ can buy a pet.
- ✔ can be sentenced to secure custody for serious or persistent offending.

From the age of 13 a young person

✔ can get a part-time job. Each area has its own bye-laws which control the type and hours of part-time work.

From the age of 14 a young person

✔ may buy soft drinks, but not alcohol, in a bar. (The licensee does not have to serve anyone and may prefer not to serve a young person under 18. Children under 14 may be in a bar which has a special Children's Licence.)

From the age of 14 a boy

✔ can be convicted of rape or unlawful sexual intercourse with a girl who is under 16.

From the age of 15 a young person

✔ may watch category 15 films.
✔ may open a Post Office Giro account or a cheque account with some banks, but an adult must agree to cover any debts.
✔ may be held in a Young Offender Institution if found guilty of an offence.

From the age of 15 a boy

✔ can be held in custody while waiting for his case to be heard in court.

From the age of 15 and 9 months a young person

✔ may join the Army Foundation College, which is the Junior Army.
✔ may join the Air Force. (Both the Army and the Air Force encourage young people to get their GCSEs before joining.)

From the age of 16 a young person

✔ may marry with a parent's or guardian's agreement.

✔ may leave school and begin full-time work, although certain jobs are still forbidden.

✔ may join the Royal Navy.

✔ can agree to dental or medical treatment (including contraception) without a parent's or guardian's permission. In certain circumstances, doctors may treat a younger person without a parent's or guardian's permission.

✔ may buy cigarettes, tobacco, liqueur chocolates and premium bonds.

✔ cannot be fostered, unless she or he is disabled.

✔ may buy beer, cider or perry served with a meal, but not in the bar of a public house.

✔ may purchase solvent-based products. (It is not illegal for a person under this age to possess solvents, but it is illegal for any shop to sell solvent-based products to a person who is, or appears to be, under 16.)

✔ may hold a licence to drive a moped or motorcycle under 50 c.c., mowing machine, invalid car and certain tractors.

✔ can legally agree to sexual intercourse.

✔ may take part in a homosexual relationship in private and provided his partner is also 16 or over. This applies to men only, as lesbianism is not recognised in law.

From the age of 17 a young person

✔ can hold a licence to drive most vehicles except heavy lorries and buses.

✔ can fly a private plane and apply for a helicopter pilot's licence.

✔ if accused of a criminal offence, is tried in a magistrates' or Crown Court, rather than in a juvenile court.

✔ can no longer be taken into care.

✔ may have his or her name added to the electoral register.

✔ may give blood. (This age limit is set by the Blood Transfusion Service and not by law.)

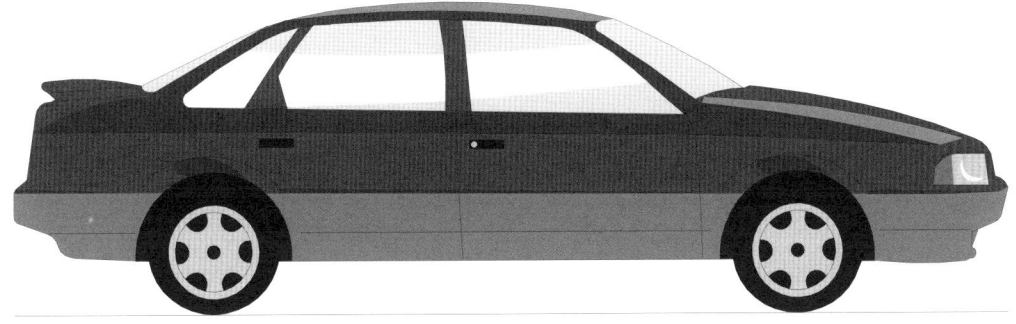

From the age of 18 a young person

✔ may marry without the agreement of a parent or guardian.

✔ cannot, if disabled, be fostered any longer.

✔ if adopted, may obtain his or her original birth certificate from the Registrar General.

✔ may make a bet in a betting shop.

✔ may see a category 18 film.

✔ may buy goods on hire-purchase or credit, and apply for a mortgage.

✔ may buy his or her own land and stocks and shares.

✔ may make a will. (A person on active military service or working at sea can make a will before the age of eighteen.)

✔ may sit as a member of a jury.

✔ may vote in local and general elections.

✔ may buy alcohol and fireworks.

✔ may join the Air Force as an Officer (providing they have the requisite qualifications).

From the age of 21 an adult

✔ may stand for election to the local council or Parliament.

✔ may, if married, adopt a child.

✔ can be sentenced to prison.

✔ may hold a licence to sell alcohol.

✔ may hold a licence to drive a lorry or bus.

RIGHT OR WRONG?

AS WE GROW UP OUR NEEDS AND WANTS CHANGE.

Look at the pictures, and decide whether each young person should have what he or she is asking for.

How do you think they should persuade their mum or dad that they are right?

UNIT 3

DO ANIMALS HAVE RIGHTS?

This unit helps students to

◆ examine the legal and moral responsibilities of keeping an animal as a pet;

◆ consider the obligations of pet owners both towards their animals and members of the public;

◆ examine issues surrounding animal rights and how these are publicly debated.

TOPIC ONE

FOR BETTER AND FOR WORSE

AIM

◆ To encourage students to think about the legal and moral responsibilities of keeping an animal as a pet.

BACKGROUND

The topic is designed as a starting point for the unit by indicating some of the responsibilities involved in the care and upkeep of pet animals.

The main law concerned with cruelty to animals is the **Protection of Animals Act 1911**. Under this Act it is an offence for anyone to:

- cruelly beat, terrify or ill-treat an animal;
- cause unnecessary suffering to an animal by wantonly or deliberately doing or omitting to do an act;
- abandon an animal in circumstances that will cause unnecessary suffering;
- use animals for the purpose of fighting.

If the owner of an animal is found guilty of cruelty under the **Protection of Animals Act 1911**, a court may deprive that person of the ownership of the animal. There are about 2,000 convictions each year for cruelty to animals. About 60 per cent of these are for cruelty to dogs.

Under the **Protection of Animals (Amendment) Act 1988** courts also have the power to prohibit a person from having custody of any animal.

Although children may keep pets, under the **Pet Animals Act 1951**, the sale of pets to children under the age of 12 is forbidden.

Local authorities may designate certain streets where a dog must be on a lead. An owner who allows a dog to roam off the lead on these roads can be fined up to £200.

Every dog on the highway or in a public place must wear a collar bearing a tag with the owner's name and address. If a dog is found on the highway or in a public place without a collar, the owner or the person in charge of the dog may be subject to a fine of up to £5,000. (This is on level five of the standard scale, a set of five payment bands, of which level five is the highest. The bands are updated every few years in line with inflation.) Anyone who finds a stray dog must either return it to its owner or report it to the police. If the dog is not claimed, the finder may, if he or she wishes, be allowed to keep the animal.

Under the **Environmental Protection Act 1990** all local councils must collect stray dogs. The owners have up to seven days to reclaim their pets, after which the animals can be found new homes or placed in the care of a rescue organisation. The local authority can charge the owners with the costs of looking after the dogs.

THE LESSON

1.   Small groups

Read the fact boxes under the heading **ANIMAL MAGIC** (page 51). Ask students to list the advantages and disadvantages of keeping animals as pets - from both a human and an animal's point of view. (Students could work individually at first, and then in pairs.)

2.   **Class discussion**

Ask students to share their ideas with the rest of the class. List these on a blackboard or OHP.

Read **HOME OR ASTRAY?** (page 51), which points to the consequences of the large number of dogs being left by their owners to roam the streets. Discuss the problem of stray dogs and ask students to think of ways in which the problem might be tackled. Would it help, for example, if the legal penalties were increased for allowing dogs to roam free?

3.   **A story**

Read the story **TIGER'S TALE** (page 52), in which students are introduced to one of the main animal welfare laws, the **Protection of Animals Act 1911**. Ask them to decide whether this law has been broken in the case outlined, and if so, to suggest what punishment should be given. Allow pupils to compare ideas and then provide them with the results of the case.

Tell students that the story is based upon a 1988 court case. Despite pleading not guilty, Anna, the accused, was fined £200 for allowing the cat to suffer unnecessarily, and ordered to pay £195 towards the costs of the case.

(The maximum penalties for this and other criminal offences are generally higher in the UK than elsewhere in Europe - but judges in the UK rarely impose the maximum sentence.)

(TOPIC TWO)

FOUL!

AIM

◆ **To encourage pupils to consider the health and environmental hazards of dogs fouling in public areas and to assess the feasibility and fairness of measures to reduce the problem.**

BACKGROUND

In recent years there has been increasing concern that children may suffer eye damage from the roundworm larvae present in the excrement of some dogs. In this topic pupils are asked to consider what can and should be done about the problem.

Toxocariasis is the disease caused when the eggs of the roundworm *toxocara canis* or *toxocara catis* are ingested by humans. Once swallowed, the microscopic eggs hatch into larvae which penetrate the wall of the intestine and travel to different parts of the body where they burrow into tissue and eventually die. It is believed that infection most commonly comes from grassed public areas, and studies show contamination in a large proportion of Britain's parks. Because of their play patterns, children are at risk.

The disease can cause a variety of disorders including stomach pains, sickness, liver damage and in a small number of cases, blindness. It is difficult to know exactly how many people are affected by the disease as, unlike some other countries, it is not notifiable in Britain. Studies, reported in the *British Medical Journal* and *The Lancet*, indicate that two to three per cent of the population show immunological evidence of past infection, with a higher rate (approximately four per cent) amongst children. In 1988, two cases of children from Blackpool who had contracted the disease were extensively reported in the press. One child lost the sight in one eye and the other in both eyes. Most reports now suggest that about 100 cases of severe eye damage, mainly amongst children are attributed to toxocariasis each year.

Despite the publicity given in recent years to the disease, there continue to be problems associated with dogs fouling public areas. 24 per cent of soil samples from public parks have been found to contain *toxocara* eggs. Under the **Dogs (Fouling of Land) Act 1996**, owners must clean up after dogs which foul on public land. Owners seen breaking this law can be served with an on-the-spot fine of £25. Failure to pay this could result in a maximum fine of £1,000.

THE LESSON

1. A newspaper story

Read **NO DOGS IN THE PARK** (page 53) and the accompanying facts about the public health problems associated with dog excrement. Go through these with the class. Ask the students if they were already aware of them and whether they feel there is a problem locally. Ask for the reaction of those students whose family has a dog and emphasise the importance of personal hygiene for those people who have pets and all who come into contact with them.

2. Small groups

Read the responses to the problem presented under the heading **TAKING ACTION** on page 54. Check that students understand each one. Explain that each person has four marks to allocate to the five points of view. For example, all four can be given to one statement, or the marks can be shared evenly between four statements. When they have done this, students should add up the scores for their group and then, with your help, determine the views of the whole class.

3.   **Class discussion**

Make sure you leave time to discuss the results. Take the most favoured option and ask pupils to consider how this might be implemented. One way would be to ask them to list the easy and difficult aspects of implementation. Concentrate on the problems and ask for suggestions how these may be overcome. Try to draw out the practical points relating to cost, public support and policing, in order to stress the importance of social and economic factors in the implementation of law.

For information on the situation locally, contact your local health authority's environmental health department.

OUT OF CONTROL?

AIMS

◆   **To assess the level of responsibility that should be accepted by owners for the animals in their charge;**

◆   **To find a just outcome to a case of an attack by a number of dogs on a young boy;**

◆   **To introduce the role of the legal system in providing a remedy for injuries received.**

BACKGROUND

Out of Control? is based upon an attack on a little boy by three dogs in the summer of 1989. The story is told through the three central characters: five-year-old Matthew Davidson, the victim; Mrs Davidson, his mother; and Mr Garner, the owner of the dogs. Pupils are asked to determine the facts of the case and to decide upon a fair outcome.

Legislation applying to dangerous dogs is found under several statutes. It is an offence under the **Town Police Clauses Act 1847** to allow any unmuzzled ferocious dog to be at large, or to urge any animal to attack or put any person or animal in fear.

The **Dogs Act 1871** gives courts the power to direct that a dog be kept under proper control by the owner or that it be destroyed. Under the **Dangerous Dogs Acts (1989 and 1991)** a court may also make an order banning a person from having custody of a dog.

The **Dangerous Dogs Act 1991** was created as a result of public concern over the number of attacks on people by fighting dogs. Under the Act it is an offence to allow any dog to be dangerously out of control in a public place.

Four breeds of dog are controlled by the Act. The pit bull terrier, the Japanese Tosa, the Dogo Argentino, and the Fila Braziliero. Owners of these dogs are forbidden to breed from the dog, advertise, sell or exchange the dog, give the dog as a gift or allow it to stray. Whenever it is in a public place, the dog should be muzzled, on a lead and in the charge of someone who is at least 16 years old. All dogs in this category must be neutered or spayed, tattooed with a special number, carry an implanted identity microchip and be covered by third party insurance.

THE LESSON

1.   ## Small groups

The students' first task is to piece together the details of the incident. Statements from each of the three main characters are collected under the heading **A NASTY INCIDENT** (pages 55 and 56). Give a set of these statements to each group of three pupils. Ask them to take one slip each, to read it in silence and then to share the information with the others in their group. Discourage pupils from exchanging slips or reading out what is on their piece of paper. When they have pieced together the whole story ask them to make a note of the main points.

2.   ## An alternative approach

Divide the class into two (assuming a class size of 25 to 30 pupils). In each half, appoint three pupils to take on the roles of Matthew, his mother and Mr Garner, and divide the remainder into three groups of three or four. The small groups now interview each of the witnesses in turn. When this has been completed, pupils use the information they have gained to answer the questions on page 57.

In real life, the court had to decide whether Mr Garner should be found guilty of 'allowing an unmuzzled ferocious dog to be at large' under the **Town Police Clauses Act 1847**. A person found guilty of this offence may be fined up to £1,000 (level three on the standard scale). Each group should decide if Mr Garner is guilty. If he is, they must also decide on a punishment and whether any or all of the dogs should be destroyed. Give pupils time to compare answers and then give them the verdict reached by the court.

In the case on which this example was based, Mr Garner was found guilty. Before passing sentence, the three magistrates heard that the same dogs had attacked a man a year before. On that occasion Mr Garner was fined £225 (£75 for each offence). They decided that he should again be fined £75 for each offence and should also pay Matthew £1,000 damages for the injuries he had received. The police made an application under the **Dogs Act 1871** for the three dogs to be destroyed and this was granted.

Ask students for their reactions and encourage them to consider the justice of the verdicts, for Matthew, Mr Garner and his dogs.

Tell students that, if the incident were to occur today Mr Garner would, if found guilty, under the **Dangerous Dogs Act 1991** now face a prison sentence of up to two years and/or a fine of up to £5,000 (level five).

TOPIC FOUR

FARMS NOT FACTORIES

AIM

> To encourage students to consider some of the legal and moral issues surrounding factory farming.

THE LESSON

1.   Class discussion

Read through the information sheets **FARMS NOT FACTORIES** (pages 58 to 59) and ask students to extract the key points on both sides of the debate before opening up a general discussion. Encourage reflective thinking by asking the class to consider some issues in more detail, such as what makes it possible for people to treat animals in ways which others feel to be so cruel. Consider the role of public awareness in this issue, asking whether the situation would be the same if the public generally knew more about factory farming conditions.

2.   A survey

Students could carry out a survey amongst their parents and other adults to discover how aware they are of typical factory conditions. The same questionnaire could be used to discover how many people know about the RSPCA's *Freedom Food* scheme.

Conditions under which other animals are often farmed could be researched by students who wish to go into this subject in more detail. The RSPCA and Compassion in World Farming both have excellent websites and provide useful educational material. See the **RESOURCES** section on page 50 for more information.

3.   **Small groups**

Ask students to consider the different ways in which countries campaigning against animal cruelty can get their messages across. These include advertising campaigns, protest marches, materials for schools, letters to MPs and consumer campaigns to buy 'cruelty free' products. Students could rank these in order of effectiveness.

CAMPAIGNING FOR CHANGE

AIM

♦ **To use the case study of the RSPCA to understand more about the way a voluntary organisation works, especially in relation to the state and statutory sources of income.**

BACKGROUND

The Royal Society for the Prevention of Cruelty to Animals was one of Britain's first charities. It was founded in 1824 in support of the **Animal Protection Act 1822** which was the world's first legislation against animal cruelty. The Society for the Prevention of Cruelty to Animals, as it was first called (it became Royal in 1840 by permission of Queen Victoria) was in fact the first law enforcement agency in the UK, predating the first police forces by several years. The RSPCA today has both a direct 'hands on' approach to the prevention of cruelty and it combines this with positive care facilities alongside educational and lobbying activities. It now works nationally and internationally, with a force of over 300 inspectors and a small army of volunteers. Its income annually now tops £60m, not a penny of which comes from the government.

THE LESSON

1.   **Class discussion**

Point out that the previous work has introduced students to the work of the RSPCA, a charity working to eliminate cruelty to animals wherever this might occur. Encourage students to consider the information contained in **A DAY IN THE LIFE OF AN INSPECTOR** (page 60). Ask students which of these tasks appears the most important and what would happen if there were no inspector on the ground to react to events.

2.   **A quiz**

The simple quiz on page 61 can be used to stimulate interest about the RSPCA itself and generate curiosity about the size of its operations. The answers to the quiz are: 1a; 2b; 3c; 4b; 5b.

The questions below the quiz can be used to stimulate discussion about the role of charities and other non-governmental organisations in changing society for the better. Questions to consider include: why it can be better for such organisations to be independent of government? On the other hand, if the charity is generally recognised by all to be doing a vital job, should not the government accept responsibility for the work? Ask students to consider what might happen if the RSPCA became an arm of the state.

TOPIC SIX

THE ROW ABOUT BANNING HUNTING WITH DOGS

AIMS

◆   **To use the Parliamentary debates in 2000 about banning hunting with dogs (with particular reference to fox hunting) to show students how Parliament typically deals with such issues;**

◆   **To show how MPs can be seen to be working in a national context with pressures being brought to bear both directly and indirectly by public opinion and the activities of pressure groups.**

BACKGROUND

Before the General Election in 1997, the Labour Party promised a free vote on the issue of hunting with dogs in its manifesto. When it was elected, the names of all its back bench MPs went into a ballot. The winners would have the chance to introduce a Private Members' Bill. One of the winners was Michael Foster MP who introduced a **Wild Mammals (Hunting with**

Dogs) Bill. Most Private Members' Bills do not become law especially if the government does not support the idea. In this case, the government said it would make time for the Bill to be debated.

There was a lot of support for the Bill amongst MPs and some large charities got together to form the Campaign for the Protection of Hunted Animals (CPHA). The RSPCA was a leading member of CPHA along with the League against Cruel Sports and the International Fund for Animal Welfare. Public opinion was also strongly in favour of banning hunting: 76% were in favour of a ban in 1997.

When MPs came to debate the Hunting with Dogs Bill in 2000, the Private Member's Bill had been taken over by the government. The government decided to offer a political compromise and gave MPs a number of options to vote on, rather than ask them to say 'yes' or 'no' to a total ban. The three choices were:

a) ban hunting with dogs,
b) allow hunters to regulate their own sport, through a new body called the Independent Supervisory Authority for Hunting (ISAH),
c) bring hunting with dogs under stricter state control (the 'middle way').

The Labour Home Secretary said that he favoured option c). Some felt that this was in the hope of calming down the opposition. However, MPs voted by 399 votes to 155 to ban hunting. Hundreds of fox hunters around the country held rallies and vowed to defy the law if a ban was brought in. This would create a great public nuisance, would cost the taxpayers a lot of money and divert the police from more important tasks. A Conservative spokesman said the ban would turn thousands of law-abiding people into criminals and do nothing to improve animal welfare.

The Bill went to the House of Lords to be debated in January 2001. The Lords voted by over 4 to 1 against a total ban and also against the 'middle way'.

It is rare for the Lords to continue opposing the Commons indefinitely, but on this issue, feelings ran very high and the Bill was delayed sufficiently so as to have run out of time when the general election was called in June 2001. It is not possible to carry on with a Bill into the next Parliament, so the government had to announce plans in its manifesto, to introduce the Bill all over again. When Tony Blair was re-elected, his government announced that it would reintroduce legislation to provide a free vote on the issue. It was thought likely that, if opposition from the Lords continued, then the **Parliament Acts** of 1911 and 1949 would be invoked. These Acts together provide that the Lords can delay ordinary Bills for no more than one complete session in a Parliament. (Note: the **Parliament Act** of 1911 took away the power of the Lords to delay money bills and severely limited their ability to veto other legislation that the Commons has passed.)

THE LESSON

1. Class discussion

This issue is both emotive and complicated. Whilst one can fairly easily be in favour of or against fox hunting, the arguments on both sides quickly become complex and factual. You could demonstrate this with the class by initiating a debate on fox hunting with little preparation. Most students will be aware of what it is and most will probably be able to say whether they are broadly in favour, against or undecided. At this point, you could invite discussion, noting the arguments which students draw on. Note too the contested points or those which are avoided by the class eg, 'how much does the fox suffer?' or 'how important is it to keep foxes under control anyway?'

At this point you could ask students to read **A VERY POLITICAL DEBATE** (pages 62 and 63) and introduce the summary of the factual finding of the Burns Report (page 63), pointing out that the government set up this enquiry precisely to shed light on the issue in the face of many competing claims. Ask if any of the findings have helped students themselves make up, or change, their minds.

2. A case study

You could discuss how the Hunting Bill was handled by the Blair government of 1997 to 2001 to give your students some idea of the workings of Parliament (see **BACKGROUND** pages 48 and 49). Point out that the Commons was overwhelmingly in favour of the ban, but was blocked by the more conservative House of Lords. You could use this to discuss the value and make up of the second chamber, especially when it directly opposes the elected chamber.

RESOURCES

The Royal Society for the Prevention of Cruelty to Animals (contact details: RSPCA Education, Wilberforce Way, Southwater, Horsham, West Sussex, RH13 7WN, Tel: 0870 010 1181 or www.rspca.org.uk), publishes information and materials on the responsibilities of pet ownership. Summaries of current legislation relating to the care and welfare of animals are also available from the RSPCA.

Compassion in World Farming (www.ciwf.co.uk) campaigns peacefully for better treatment of farm animals. They produce scientific reports and gather undercover evidence on animal suffering.

Advice and information on the extent of *toxicara canis* in your own area, and measures taken to deal with the fouling of public places, may be obtained from the offices of the local environmental health and highways divisions. They can also supply copies of local bye-laws.

FOR BETTER AND FOR WORSE

ANIMAL MAGIC

PEOPLE LOVE PETS! ABOUT HALF THE FAMILIES IN BRITAIN HAVE A PET.

PET CATS KILL BIRDS AND SMALL ANIMALS IN SUCH LARGE NUMBERS THAT THEY ARE HAVING A SERIOUS IMPACT ON LEVELS OF WILDLIFE.

I WISH MORE PEOPLE WOULD CLEAR UP THEIR DOGS' MESS – IT'S A REAL WORRY.

I LIVE ALONE; I RELY ON MY DOG FOR COMPANIONSHIP.

MORE THAN 7,000,000 DOGS (THAT'S SEVEN MILLION!) AND 5,000,000 CATS ARE KEPT AS PETS IN BRITAIN.

Draw up a list of the points for and against keeping animals as pets. Share your list with a friend and choose between you the three best things and the three most difficult things about keeping a pet.

If animals could talk, what do you think they might say were the three best and worst things about being kept as a pet?

HOME OR ASTRAY?

Did you know ... ?

- At any one time, about half a million dogs are left by their owners to roam the streets.
- Because many owners abandon their dogs, about 1,000 dogs, many quite healthy, are put down every day.
- Stray dogs are thought to cause about 54,000 road accidents a year, in which over 1,000 people are injured.
- Stray dogs also cause problems on farms. Every year about 10,000 farm animals are attacked. The cost of this is thought to be more than £1 million.

What do you think can be done about the problem of stray dogs? Do you think the law should be changed in any way? Should it be harder to own a dog?

TIGER'S TALE

One night, Naina Prashad found a cat lying on her doorstep.
It was Tiger, who belonged to Anna, Naina's next-door neighbour.

The cat looked very weak, so Naina took it in overnight, caring for it as best she could. In the morning Naina took Tiger back to Anna and told her to take the cat to a vet.

That evening, Tiger was on Naina's doorstep again. He was looking worse. His stomach was badly swollen and he could hardly walk. Naina took Tiger round to Anna's and told her that she must call the vet straight away. Anna said that she was busy, and told Naina to stop interfering. Naina gave the cat to Anna and left.

In the morning, Tiger was back. Naina decided that she had to do something herself. She called the RSPCA and then took the animal to a vet. The vet said that Tiger was suffering from cancer and would have to be put down. The RSPCA called the police, and Anna was charged with allowing the animal to suffer unnecessarily.

WHAT THE LAW SAYS

The main law protecting animals is the Protection of Animals Act 1911.

Under this law it is an offence to cause an animal to suffer unnecessarily. A person found guilty of unnecessary cruelty or neglect of an animal can be fined up to £5,000 or sent to prison for up to three months.

FOUL!

A Sting in the Tail

Dogs are good friends to millions of people. But many dogs have small worms living inside them whose eggs, when swallowed by humans, can cause serious illness.

NO DOGS IN THE PARK

THE BOROUGH council in Burnley, Lancashire, has banned dogs - even if they are on a lead - from all parks in the town.

Said a council official: 'We had a lot of complaints about dogs fouling in public parks and we decided that banning dogs (except guide dogs) from the park was the best way to deal with the problem'.

THESE ARE THE FACTS:

◆ Out of every five dogs, about three have a roundworm inside them called *toxocara canis*.

◆ The eggs of the worm pass out of the dog, in the animal's excreta.

◆ These eggs can be found on the ground in many parks and open spaces where dogs are exercised.

◆ It is hard to get rid of the eggs. They stay alive on the ground for up to two years.

◆ Children who play on grass where these microscopic eggs have been left may accidentally swallow them. The eggs hatch into larvae which travel through the bloodstream to different parts of the body.

◆ The larvae can cause illness, damage to the eyes and even blindness. It is believed that each year between 50 and 100 children's eyesight is damaged by the disease.

WHAT THE LAW SAYS

Most local councils have a law which states that it is an offence to allow a dog to foul a public footpath or grass verge. Anyone found guilty of this may be fined up to £100.

TAKING ACTION

A   NO DOGS ALLOWED

> OWNERS SHOULD NOT BE ALLOWED TO TAKE A DOG INTO PARKS OR FIELDS WHERE CHILDREN PLAY.

B   IT'S NOT A PROBLEM

> PEOPLE ARE TOO FUSSY. IT'S NOT A SERIOUS PROBLEM.

C   SAFE DISPOSAL

> OWNERS SHOULD BE RESPONSIBLE FOR SAFELY GETTING RID OF THEIR DOG'S EXCREMENT.

D   HAVE YOUR DOG CHECKED

> OWNERS SHOULD HAVE THEIR DOG CHECKED BY A VET EVERY SIX MONTHS.

E   INCREASE THE FINES

> DOG OWNERS WHO ALLOW THEIR DOGS TO LEAVE EXCREMENT IN PUBLIC PLACES SHOULD BE HEAVILY FINED.

You each have four marks available. You can award these to the opinions as you like, but don't give half or quarter marks.
So if you only agree with C, then you might give all four marks to that statement. But if you think B and D are the best ideas, then you would probably give two marks to each one.

When you have made your own decision, add together the marks given to each opinion by the people in your group. What is your group's first choice?

OUT OF CONTROL?

A Nasty Incident

MATTHEW DAVIDSON'S STORY ...

"My name is Matthew. I'm five years old. Last Sunday I went out on my bike with my Mum. I was riding along when some dogs ran out and knocked me over. One of them kept biting me and wouldn't let go. It hurt a lot. My Mum got the dogs away and I was taken to hospital in an ambulance. I had to stay in hospital and lots of doctors and nurses looked after me. Mum says I've got 21 stitches in my arm, my leg and my tummy."

MRS DAVIDSON'S STORY ...

"Matthew was riding his bike just ahead of me. A man was on the other side of the road with three large dogs. None of them was on a lead. I watched the dogs run across the road. They went straight for Matthew and knocked him off his bike. One of the dogs got hold of his arm and tossed him in the air like a piece of meat. He looked like a rag doll, all covered in blood. if I hadn't managed to pull Matthew away, he would have been eaten alive."

"The owner got hold of the dogs and pushed them into his van which was parked nearby. And that was it. Without a word, he just drove off."

MR GARNER'S STORY ...

"I like dogs. I have had Archie for more than three years. He's a lovely family pet. Dan and Digger are his puppies. I need them to guard my house. I have a market stall and I keep my stock in a shed in the back yard. There are lots of burglaries around here. Nothing's safe."

"I'd just taken the dogs for a walk in the park. They had been no bother, so I let them stay off the lead till we got back to the van. The little boy was shouting, pretending to drive a racing car. I think that's what made them go for him. I got the dogs in the van as soon as I could. I knew the boy would be all right, but I was scared that the police would be called and I'd have to have the dogs put down. It's just because they are Rottweilers. The next day the story was in the papers, so I went to the police and gave myself up. They said they would try to get the dogs destroyed. I thought that was wrong, so when I got home I arranged for Dan and Digger to be given away."

GETTING SOMETHING DONE

A little boy has been attacked by dogs and injured. The owner of the dogs, Mr Garner, has been charged with breaking **Dangerous Dogs Act 1991**, which says that it is an offence to allow an unmuzzled ferocious dog to be free and out of control. The police have also asked the court to order the dogs to be destroyed.

Work out what happened by reading the three accounts of the incident.

Now you are one of the magistrates in court. You must decide four things:

1. Is Mr Garner guilty of allowing an unmuzzled ferocious dog to be at large?
2. If Mr Garner is guilty, should he pay Matthew some money in compensation for the injuries he received? Mr Garner's income is £20,000 per year.
3. If Mr Garner is guilty, should he be fined? The maximum fine is £1000.
4. Should Archie, Dan and Digger be destroyed? What are the arguments for and against this?

WHAT THE LAW SAYS

THE LAW CHANGES

After a series of attacks on children and adults by dogs, the Dangerous Dogs Act 1991 was passed making it illegal to allow any dog to be dangerously out of control in a public place.

The Act also makes it illegal to breed or sell pit bull terriers, Japanese Tosa, the Dogo Argentino and the Fila Braziliero. These dogs should be on a lead and muzzled when in a public place and in the charge of someone who is at least 16 years old. Rottweilers are not on the list of specially controlled dogs.

FARMS NOT FACTORIES
FARMING AND ANIMAL WELFARE

Most people prefer their food to be cheap, but people may not realise that this can mean a great deal of suffering for animals. One of the best examples of this is the battery hen system, which animal welfare organisations have been campaigning against for many years. The more hens that can be crammed into a space, the cheaper it becomes to produce the eggs. Often up to five hens are packed inside each battery cage. They cannot behave naturally, being unable to stretch their wings, or perch or scratch at the ground for food. It can be said that this method of farming treats these animals more like things than living creatures in their own right.

Other chickens are bred for their meat. These are called broiler chickens. In this case, they are allowed to move around but thousands of birds are kept in very crowded barns and the hens are bred to grow twice as fast as is natural. This causes problems because their young legs are not strong enough to carry the extra weight.

Animal campaigners, such as The Royal Society for the Prevention of Cruelty to Animals (RSPCA) and Compassion in World Farming (CIWF) have tried to raise public awareness of these issues for years. Perhaps because of some major health scares, such as the BSE outbreak in beef, people are beginning to change their attitudes and are asking questions about how their food is produced. This is not always easy to discover. For

example, the words 'Farm Fresh' eggs sound healthy but are likely to have come from battery hens. The term 'Barn eggs' (which sounds better) says nothing about how over-crowded the barns are.
The RSPCA has responded to consumer concern by setting up its 'Freedom Food' scheme. Eggs produced under the scheme are guaranteed to come from chickens with enough room to move around easily and to scratch and perch naturally.

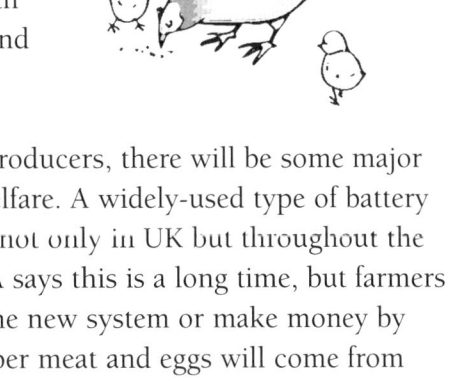

After a great deal of opposition from producers, there will be some major changes to the law affecting animal welfare. A widely-used type of battery cage is being replaced by larger cages, not only in UK but throughout the European Union, by 2012. The RSPCA says this is a long time, but farmers say they need time to switch over to the new system or make money by other means. Their worry is that cheaper meat and eggs will come from outside the European Union where conditions are less strictly controlled. They believe this could drive them out of business because most consumers will still care more about the price than the conditions in which the food was produced.

What are the arguments for and against factory farming methods? How good are these arguments in your view?

◆ **Why is it important that charities campaigning against animal cruelty know how to 'get their message across'? What methods do you think are best for this? They could include:**

- **advertising campaigns**
- **protest marches**
- **materials for schools**
- **writing to MPs**
- **consumer campaigns to buy 'cruelty free' products.**

◆ **Research other 'cruelty free' products. What are they? How important is it that consumers have a choice? What kinds of products should be allowed to be tested on animals, in your opinion, and why?**

◆ **People often say that they can't make a difference on their own so they don't get involved. How good an argument is this?**

CAMPAINING FOR CHANGE

A DAY IN THE LIFE OF AN INSPECTOR

Dave Braybrooke is an RSPCA inspector in Milton Keynes. He describes what he did during one typical day:

◆ I was called to where a fox had been hit by a car. It had a broken back and I put it to sleep.

◆ I rescued a cat stuck in a tree. The cat was unharmed.

◆ I then picked up a stray cat with kittens found in the street and took them to the local RSPCA branch to be looked after.

◆ I answered a call which claimed some horses were tangled up in the ropes which were tethering them. One of the horses bit me, although I was being careful.

◆ After that I checked a complaint that some rabbits were being kept in filthy cages. This is common. The rabbits were OK but their bedding needed changing and they had no water or fresh food.

◆ I then went to inspect a German Shepherd dog in poor condition and give the owners some advice on treating the animal for fleas.

◆ I investigated the conditions in which a North American Corn Snake was being kept. I decided the animal was not being well looked after and I took it away to be checked and rehomed.

Imagine that all these requests for help and complaints came in at the same time, early in the day. If you were the inspector, in which order would you attend to these incidents?

What qualities do you think you would need to be an RSPCA inspector like Dave Braybrooke? What do you think are the rewards of doing a job like this and what are the difficulties involved?

THE ROYAL SOCIETY FOR THE PREVENTION OF CRUELTY TO ANIMALS

There are many charities which exist to improve conditions for animals but one of the oldest and the biggest is the RSPCA. Everyone has heard of the RSPCA but this doesn't mean they know much about it.

Here are a few statements about the RSPCA. Which of the answers do you think correctly completes each statement?

1.   **The RSPCA was founded in:**
     a) 1824
     b) 1947

2.   **The RSPCA receives funding from:**
     a) the public and the government
     b) only the public
     c) only the government

3.   **In 1999, the RSPCA's income was:**
     a) £20m
     b) £30m
     c) £60m

4.   **In 1999 the RSPCA prosecuted (took to court):**
     a) more people for cruelty to cats than dogs
     b) more people for cruelty to dogs than for cats, horses and pigs put together

     In 1999 the RSPCA prosecuted
     a) about 500 people
     b) about 1,000 people
     c) about 1,250 people

☆   **The RSPCA receives a huge amount of support from the public, but isn't this a job the state should be doing? What would be the arguments for and against this point of view?**

THE ROW ABOUT BANNING HUNTING WITH DOGS

A VERY POLITICAL DEBATE

People often say politics is boring whilst at the same time getting very involved in political arguments. A good example of this is the debate about banning hunting with dogs. Large numbers of people on both sides of the argument have become involved in very heated discussions. The debate is political because it is about how we run the country.

WHAT IS THE ROW ABOUT?

Hunting wild animals with dogs has gone on for a long time in this country. It has become part of some people's way of life and their means of earning a living. The fox is the most widely hunted animal but dogs are also used in hunting wild deer, hares and mink. Supporters claim that hunting is about keeping down the number of foxes who kill chicken and sheep but hunts (the organisations which own the dogs) do make sure that foxes have somewhere to live in their area so that on hunting days, there is plenty of good sport.

Opponents say that hunting for sport is wrong and that there are less cruel ways of controlling the fox population. They claim that fox hunting is a 'medieval' practice like bear-baiting and cock-fighting which has no place in a civilised and humane society.

Many Members of Parliament, when polled, said they believe that hunting with dogs should be made illegal. One problem is that this kind of issue partly rests on people's private beliefs or consciences and on many of these issues, the government refuses to get involved. These days 'freedom of conscience' is guaranteed under the **Human Rights Act 1998** and the European Convention on Human Rights.

On the other hand, it is already against the law to inflict unnecessary suffering on any animal, so it is possible to argue that this is not about conscience or a way of life but about killing animals in a cruel way just to have some sport. In cases like this MPs are often allowed a 'free vote' according to their own beliefs and not a strict party policy.

One of the problems with the issue was that there was disagreement over key facts, including how badly animals suffer before they die. Another dispute was over how many people in the countryside would lose money and jobs if hunting were banned. The government set up an inquiry headed by Lord Burns to try to discover the truth. The inquiry took evidence from both sides and came to the opinion in the Burns' Report that:

- foxes and other animals suffered a good deal before death. They did not die instantly as some people claimed, though death quickly follows being caught by the hounds;
- shooting foxes where this is necessary is less cruel;
- a ban on hunting would not seriously increase the number of foxes in lowland areas (far more foxes are killed on the roads each year than by hunting);
- hunting with dogs accounts for just a small proportion of the foxes, deer, hares and mink which need to be killed every year as pests or to control their populations;
- about 3 per cent of lambs are taken by foxes every year;
- about 700 full-time jobs would go if hunting were banned (opponents had claimed it would be many more than this), plus another 2,000 jobs or so, which are in industries like stabling horses and selling riding equipment which partly depend on the hunts for trade. Many affected people would find other work.

THE DEBATE IN PARLIAMENT

When MPs came to debate the **Hunting with Dogs Bill** in 2000, the government decided to offer a political compromise and gave MPs a number of options to vote on, rather than ask them to say 'yes' or 'no' to a total ban. The three choices were:

a) ban hunting with dogs,

b) allow hunters to regulate their own sport, through a new body called the Independent Supervisory Authority for Hunting (ISAH),

c) bring hunting with dogs under stricter state control (the 'middle way').

Imagine you are an MP. How would you vote on this issue?

UNIT 4

CAN YOU HEAR ME?

This unit helps students to

◆ consider questions of fairness, responsibility and discipline in schools;

◆ examine the purpose of rules, and fair ways of developing and enforcing them;

◆ consider ways in which young people can make their voice heard in school and the community.

TOPIC ONE

APPLEYARD SCHOOL

AIMS

◆ To consider the problems of drafting school rules and the basis on which school rules should be framed;

◆ To show how the law extends to conduct within the school.

BACKGROUND

Appleyard School has just opened. The head teacher, Mrs Robinson, is looking for a way of minimising the number of rules relating to behaviour in school. She decides on just one rule: Do not break the law and always act considerately towards other people.

Students assess this rule in the light of a number of events which take place during the first term.

Further information about two of the incidents on the slips on page 71 may be helpful:

Spitting

As an offence, spitting at another person is quite complex. The students' sheet offers a simplified version for the sake of clarity.

● Spitting at another person may be an offence under the **Public Order Act 1986** if it causes harassment, alarm or distress to another person. Spitting may also contravene the same Act where it causes a person to fear for their personal safety, i.e. if it is done in a threatening manner.

● It is also an assault (or more accurately a battery). With a battery, physical contact with the victim has been made - strictly speaking an assault is merely putting someone in fear of being imminently harmed through the use of words or actions. Throwing an object at another has been ruled to be a battery and spitting would be seen as a similar offence.

● Spitting at someone is also a trespass to the person. This is not a crime but a tort (a civil wrong). If damage were caused as a result of the tort it would be possible in theory to sue for damages in the county court.

Teachers should be aware that the practice of spitting is regarded differently in different cultures. Amongst Muslims, who are forbidden to swallow their own saliva during Ramadan, the month of fasting, spitting is more acceptable. Some schools have encouraged Muslim pupils to use tissues rather than spit.

Racial abuse

It is stated in the students' materials that it is against the law, under the **Public Order Act 1986**, to use abusive or insulting language which causes a person to be harassed, alarmed or distressed. Incitement to racial hatred is also an offence under the same Act. In addition, under the **Race Relations Act 1976**, as amended by the **Race Relations (Amendment) Act 2000**, schools themselves have a general duty to ensure that pupils are not discriminated against by being subjected to detrimental treatment. Thus if a school failed to act against racism it would be in breach of the Act. Schools and other public bodies now also have a general duty to promote racial equality.

THE LESSON

1.   Class discussion

Give out page 71 and introduce students to the situation at Appleyard School. Ask the class to think about the point of keeping school rules to a minimum. Ask for students' initial reactions to Mrs Robinson's draft rule.

Now ask the class to look at the eight incidents and to consider the each in the light of Mrs Robinson's rule.

2.   **Small groups**

Ask students to divide the incidents into two categories - one which the rule covers (in whole or in part) and one which the rule does not cover. The sheets **TESTING MRS ROBINSON'S RULE** (pages 72 to 73) are provided for students' reference. These could be given out now or later when they have had a chance to think for themselves about what the law might say.

3.   **Class discussion**

When the incidents have been divided, go through each incident discussing whether it breaches one or other part of the rule. For example, writing on a desk may be seen as against the law and many (but perhaps not all) would also see it as an inconsiderate act towards others. Ask the class to give reasons for their views.

Now consider what is to be done about the incidents not covered by the rule. Should incidents like these be banned? If so, for what reason? If they should, then how would students alter Mrs Robinson's rule? Are more rules needed after all? Students might decide that 'victimless offences' like smoking should be dealt with by additional rules. In such cases, students should be encouraged to think about the reasons why such acts might be prohibited on school premises.

Certain practices which take place in school, such as theft, bullying and racial abuse are often dealt with by the school, using its own system of sanctions, without reference to the police or other outside bodies. Ask students what they feel about this. Should schools be quicker to involve the police in such incidents?

THAT'S THE RULE

AIM

   To consider the reasons for rules in schools.

BACKGROUND

A poem is used as the starting point to consider the reasons for school rules and assess their fairness.

It is worth ensuring that year heads and form tutors know that the exercise in consultation suggested at the end of this topic is taking place. As with other topics in this unit, the lesson might benefit from the presence of a senior member of staff who could comment on the suggestions made by students and give them the opportunity to voice their views to someone in a position to act on them. **The Elton Report on Discipline in Schools (1989)** pointed out: 'It may be clear to teachers why particular rules are necessary. It is not always clear to pupils or parents ... . Any rule for which no rational explanation can be provided is suspect.' (page 89)

THE LESSON

1.   **A poem**

Give out page 74 and read the poem *Our School* with the class.

2.   **Class discussion**

Ask students why they think the children have been asked to wait in the playground. Encourage them to reflect on the purpose of the rule and for whose benefit it has been made. Do the pupils themselves benefit from the rule in any way?

The poem indicates that the rule may have unfortunate results. If students feel that the rule is unfair, ask them how it might be made fairer. Encourage them to give reasons for their suggestions and to think about the effects the change in the rule might bring. For example, if pupils are allowed into school whenever they arrive in the morning, what might result? What does the class feel is the best compromise between the need to protect pupils and to safeguard school property?

3.   **Written work**

Ask students to list five of their school rules and suggest the reasons for them.

4.   **Class discussion**

Compile a list of all the rules mentioned and discuss whether they fall into certain categories (eg, safety). Why have other rules been made? It may emerge that some rules are not understood by students. Use this opportunity to discuss these further and to raise the question of why it is important for rules to be understood and accepted by those affected by them.

As a final task as part of this topic students are asked to consider school rules which they would like to see changed in some way. Make it clear that you are not inviting complaints but asking for constructive comments. Teachers can benefit from understanding how things feel from the students' standpoint. Naturally, this task should be handled with care.

A BETTER PLACE

AIM

◆ **To consider ways in which young people can make their voices heard in school and the community.**

BACKGROUND

This topic looks in some detail at the question of 'student democracy' in schools. It draws on data gathered by Don Rowe and published by the Citizenship Foundation in a report called *The Business of School Councils*. The report sets out the difficulties encountered by teachers and students in eight schools in their attempts to find the most effective ways of engaging in the process of school improvement. Besides the problems, the research also found many outstanding examples of students dealing effectively with serious curriculum and management issues to the benefit of the pupils and the school as a whole.

The second half of this topic offers a case study of youth social action in the community. This is a real case and the company concerned was a major household name in the sportswear field. This case study offers students the chance to understand the importance to a campaign of clear aims and appropriate strategies. It also clearly shows that self-belief, when this leads to courage and persistence, can achieve a surprising amount. The case study is taken from *Changing Places* by Ted Huddleston, published by National Youth Agency, 2000.

THE LESSON

1. Class discussion

Introduce the lesson with a brief discussion of the situation in your school. If you already have a school council, ask how many students are aware of what the council is discussing at the moment. Do students know who the form reps are, how often the council meets and so on? How many school council successes can students identify?

Many students seem to be cynical about the effectiveness of their own school council and many teachers (for example, in the research mentioned above) are seen by students as ambivalent about school councils. Why do the students think this is?

2.   **Small groups**

Give out the sheet **A BETTER PLACE** (page 75) and ask students to consider the statements made by teachers and students. To what extent do they sympathise with the positions stated? Why do they think these opinions have developed? Relate each of these statements to the situation in your own school.

3.   **Class discussion**

Gather together responses from the small group work. What other reasons might students have for thinking that school councils are not as effective as they should be? What issues would they ideally like a school council to address?

4.   **Small groups**

Give out the sheet **GETTING THINGS DONE** (page 76). Look at the summary of issues drawn from the same piece of research. It suggests that there is virtually no part of school life which cannot benefit from genuine engagement with student opinion. Ask the groups to consider the areas listed and think of issues in your school which might come under these different headings.

In their groups, students could take one issue and prepare a report on it, suggesting how things could be improved. Ask them to think about the best way to present their reports and to check whether they have as much evidence as possible to back up their case.

Use student feedback to focus, in a positive way, on how students can make a difference once they become engaged with an issue. Consider also ways in which teachers need to support students in these efforts. Is it better for school councils to work independently of staff or in close partnership with them? Opinion is divided on this question. However, the finding of the report *The Business of School Councils* is that the most successful school councils seem to be where two-way communication ('top down' and 'bottom up') is strongest.

5.   **A case study**

Use the case **THE BIG TRAINER PROTEST** (pages 77 to 79) as a good example of young people conducting a successful piece of social action. Read the example with the class and ask them individually or in pairs to underline examples of strategies or tactics adopted by the group. Why did they choose this way as opposed to some other? How well did it work? Would some other way have been possible or even more effective? Why was the company so keen to persuade the group that they had taken notice? How important was this piece of social action? Why did Hayley seem to gain so much satisfaction from it?

This piece could obviously be followed up in a number of ways. Some students might consider researching the present state of child labour in the trainer industry. Are things continuing to improve? Are there other issues that members of the class feel to be as important? What would be a good way to go about making their voice heard?

RESOURCES

Specialist information on legal aspects of education is available in *The Head's Legal Guide*, Croner Publications Limited. Many schools subscribe to this regularly updated guide to education law.

The following organisations are able to provide advice and information on legal aspects of education:

- **The Advisory Centre for Education** (ACE), 1c Aberdeen Studios, 22-24 Highbury Grove, London N5 2DQ, 0208 800 5793 www.ace-ed.org.uk/
- **The Children's Legal Centre**, University of Essex, Wivenhoe Park Colchester, Essex CO4 35Q, 01206 873820.
- The legal departments of teachers' unions and associations may also be able to help with enquiries.

The report *The Business of School Councils* by Don Rowe is available from The Citizenship Foundation (www.citfou.org.uk).

APPLEYARD SCHOOL
FINDING THE WORDS

Appleyard School has just opened. The school takes pupils from 11 to 18 years of age. Mrs Robinson, the head, wants to find a single rule to cover everyone's behaviour. So she suggests the following rule:

> **Do not break the law and always act considerately towards other people.**

Now look at the list of eight incidents which the teachers have to deal with during the first term. Divide the incidents into two categories: put a tick against those which Mrs Robinson's rule covers and a cross against those which Mrs Robinson's rule does not cover.

1 Someone has written on a desk in a classroom.	
2 A teacher notices one pupil spitting at another.	
3 Some pupils are frequently arriving late for school.	
4 Some pupils in year 9 are found smoking on the school premises at lunch time.	
5 A small group of pupils in year 8 threaten to hit two younger pupils if they do not hand over some money.	
6 A few pupils are shouting racist insults to some of the others.	
7 A teacher is encouraging pupils to call him by his first name.	
8 A pupil discovers in class that a pen in her pocket has leaked on to her shirt. She swears loudly.	

TESTING
MRS ROBINSON'S RULE

WHAT THE LAW SAYS

Schools have a legal right to set rules and punishments, as long as they are reasonable.

1 **Writing on desks**
   Under the **Criminal Damage Act 1971**, it is against the law deliberately to damage property which belongs to someone else.

2 **Spitting**
   When a person spits at someone it is known in law as an assault and battery. This is a crime. In theory the person who is spat upon may also have a case for damages for the injury to their feelings or the cost of having to have an item of their clothing cleaned. However, in practice it would not be worth going to law.

3 **Arriving late for school**
   Frequent lateness often causes inconvenience to others, and in this case is also against the law. Under the **Education Act 1944**, a parent must make sure his or her child gets to school on time. If not, the parent can be prosecuted for the child's non attendance. In the eyes of the law regular lateness at school is the same as non attendance.

4 **Smoking**
   Smoking is unhealthy, but it is not in itself an offence for a young person to smoke. However, it is an offence to sell cigarettes to children under 16 and police officers and uniformed park keepers have the right to confiscate cigarettes from young people under 16 found smoking in public.

5 **Demanding money**
   It is against the law to ask for something from someone by threatening them. In law, this is a form of blackmail.

6   **Racist insults**

This is a crime. Under the **Public Order Act 1986**, it is against the law to use abusive or insulting language in public which causes a person to be harassed, alarmed or distressed. Incitement to racial hatred is also an offence under the same Act, though prosecutions are rare. In addition, under the **Race Relations Act 1976**, as amended by the **Race Relations (Amendment) Act 2000**, schools themselves have a general duty to ensure that pupils are not discriminated against by being subjected to detrimental treatment. Thus if a school failed to act against racism it would be in breach of the Act.

7   **Using first names**

It is not against the law for teachers to allow pupils to call them by their first name.

8   **Swearing**

It is against the law to use words in a public place which are particularly abusive or might alarm or distress someone, but it is unlikely that the reaction of the pupil who discovers the stain on her shirt would be seen in this way.

THAT'S THE RULE

Our School

We have this rule at our school
You've got to wait till the whistle blows
And you can't go in till you hear it
Not even if it snows
And your wellies get filled with water and
your socks go all soggy and start
slipping down your legs
And your hands get so cold they go all
crumpled and you can't undo the buttons
on your mac when you get inside
.... it's true

Gareth Owen

Why are the children waiting in the playground?
Do you think what they are being asked to do is fair?
Would you change the rule? If so, how would you change it and why?

YOUR SCHOOL RULES

List five of your school rules and after each one say why you think the
rule has been made. Compare your list with others in the class.

Which rules would you like to change or introduce in your school? Give
reasons for your ideas and try to say how you think the changes would
improve things. How far do other people agree with you? How far do you
think teachers and parents would agree?

A BETTER PLACE

SCHOOL COUNCILS

Many schools have school councils, including primary schools. The idea of a school council is to allow students to have a say in the running of the school. Not only that, it gives them a chance to suggest ways in which their school can be made a better place.

But school councils are not all that easy to run.

Look at the following quotations from real pupils and teachers about their experiences and try to decide what, why or how the problem has arisen. Then think about ways in which the situation might be improved. Are things like this in your school?

I'VE LEARNT THAT IT'S QUITE HARD TO GET THINGS ACROSS TO THE TEACHERS AND YOU HAVE TO REALLY PUSH AT IT IF YOU WANT THINGS DONE.

SOMETIMES THEY TREAT US LIKE ADULTS BUT THEN THEY START TREATING YOU LIKE LITTLE KIDS. IT'S AN UNEVEN BALANCE - IT SUITS THEM: IT DON'T SUIT US.

IT'S A SHAME THAT THE STUDENT COUNCIL ONLY LOOKS AT WHAT WE SAY ARE THE PETTY ISSUES. BECAUSE, LET'S BE HONEST, IT IS A PETTY ISSUE WHETHER YOU CAN WEAR YOUR TIE OR NOT IN THE SUMMER. WE DON'T GET TO LOOK AT THE ONES THAT ACTUALLY DO MATTER.

IT'S NOT NORMAL PRACTICE IS IT, FOR STAFF TO GO OUT AND SAY, "TELL ME WHAT YOU THINK IS WRONG WITH ME".

WHEN I FIRST CAME HERE TEN YEARS AGO THERE WAS A STUDENT COUNCIL. IT ONLY LASTED 18 MONTHS BEFORE IT DISINTEGRATED AND I COULD SEE WHY. MANY PEOPLE WHO WERE ELECTED TO IT, DIDN'T TURN UP TO IT.

THERE ARE LOTS OF STAFF WHO I THINK WOULD FEEL QUITE THREATENED BY AN EFFECTIVE SCHOOL COUNCIL.

GETTING THINGS DONE

Some school councils – in primary and secondary schools – have done some amazing things – and age is not necessarily a problem. For example, in one primary school, a discussion about bullying by Year 3 pupils led to a questionnaire of pupils across the school to find out about how serious the problem was. This found several trouble spots and led to a big improvement in the situation. In another primary school, the pupils are involved in all kinds of things, including interviewing new members of staff.

One piece of research collected information on all the issues which had been recently discussed in just eight primary and secondary schools. The list was very long. Here are a few of the issues.

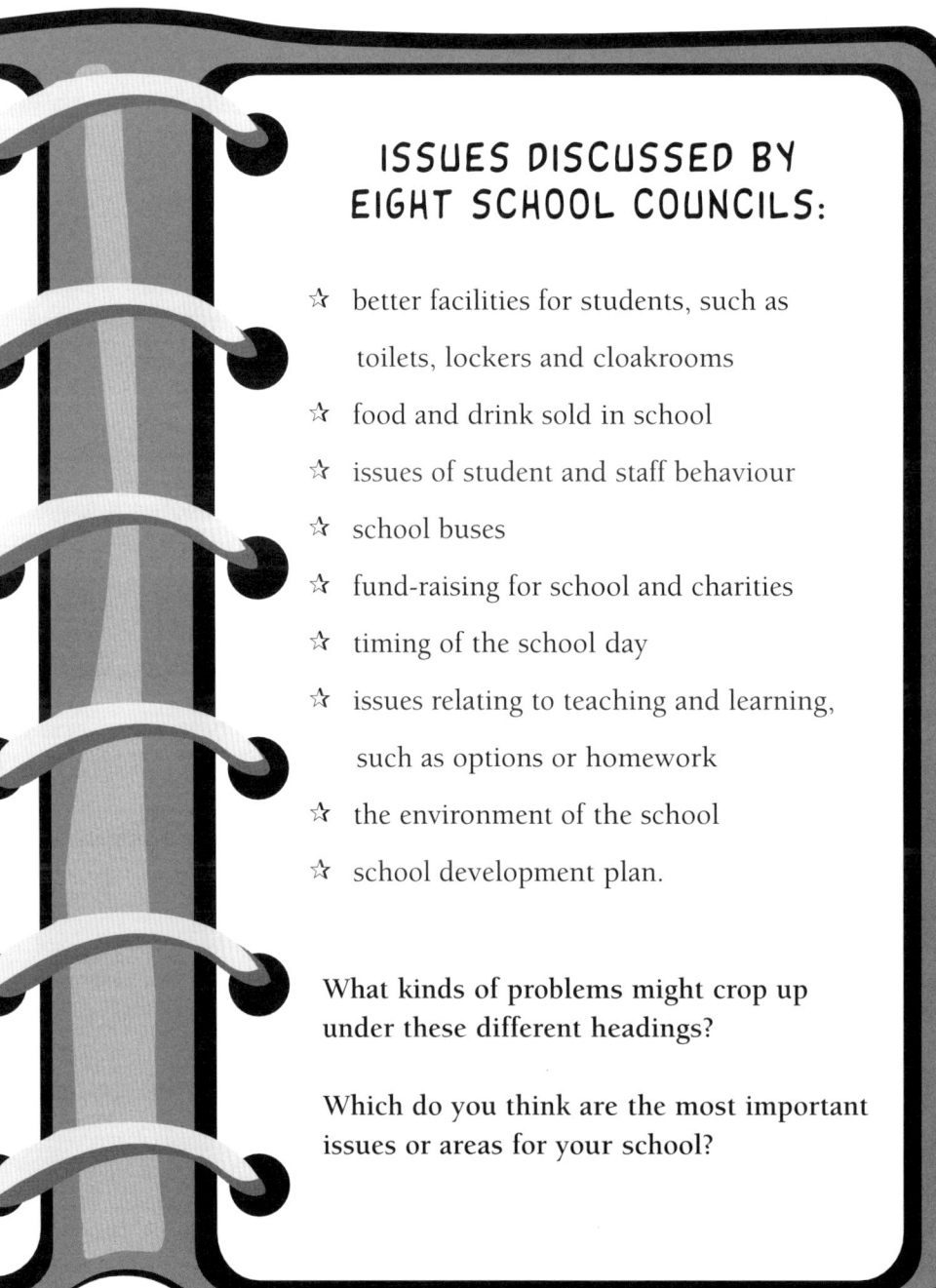

ISSUES DISCUSSED BY EIGHT SCHOOL COUNCILS:

☆ better facilities for students, such as toilets, lockers and cloakrooms

☆ food and drink sold in school

☆ issues of student and staff behaviour

☆ school buses

☆ fund-raising for school and charities

☆ timing of the school day

☆ issues relating to teaching and learning, such as options or homework

☆ the environment of the school

☆ school development plan.

What kinds of problems might crop up under these different headings?

Which do you think are the most important issues or areas for your school?

THE BIG TRAINER PROTEST

Another way of having a say in things is to protest against something you disagree with. Every citizen of this country has the right to free speech, although there are limits to how and where you can exercise this.

People who want to protest against something need to think very carefully about the best way to do it. They want to use tactics which get other people on their side and they also need to know who to protest to.

Read the example of a successful campaign to change something. Why do you think the group actually achieved something?

HAYLEY'S STORY

Hayley was 13 when she learnt to her horror about the working conditions of some children overseas who were making trainers for a well-known company. She and some friends strongly felt they wanted to do something to help. But what could they do that could possibly make a difference?

They first tried to find out as much as possible about the problem. They found a report from Christian Aid. As Hayley says,

◆ "It told about the long working hours that the workers had to endure, the dangerous chemicals they used and the dangerous operations they had to carry out."

Then they double-checked their facts.

◆ "Chris, one of the boys in the group searched the web for everything he could find out about this company. There was no doubt that what we had heard was true."

◆ "Somebody had the idea of making some postcards and asking people to sign them and send them off to the company. As we were part of a Local Agenda 21 project, the council gave us a grant to have 1,000 printed."

The wording the group settled on was:

"PLEASE CONSIDER HOW YOU ARE TREATING YOUR WORKERS AND HOW YOU ARE DEPRIVING THEM OF THEIR BASIC RIGHTS. WE BUY YOUR PRODUCTS - PLEASE ADOPT AN ETHICAL CODE OF CONDUCT FOR YOUR WORKERS & MONITOR IT INDEPENDENTLY."

But how would they get enough people to sign their postcards?

- "We were in the meeting one day just throwing some ideas about when Sophie came up with the idea:

- 'Why don't we build a big model trainer? We could take the trainer out on to the streets, and ask people to sign our postcards and drop them inside - like a kind of postbox.'

- "It took us about three Saturdays and a couple of evenings to make the giant trainer. We used papier-mache, bamboo garden canes, old chicken wire and anything else we could find. We started by drawing the shape of the bottom of the trainer on a piece of cardboard and worked from there. It was about four metres long and a metre in width. It took five or six of us to carry it."

- "Vicki's dad let us build it in his garage, which was very nice of him. But he wasn't too chuffed when it came to storing it there afterwards. It took up so much space!"

Hayley and her friends took the giant trainer into the local High Street, having first got permission. Not everyone they met there was positive.

"There is always the temptation to yell at them, 'Why can't you understand?' but there's no point if they don't want to accept it. We thought we were fighting for human rights but some people just didn't see it that way."

The group collected around 1,000 postcards and after getting nowhere with the company office in London (which admitted nothing), they decided to

send the cards in batches to the German headquarters. After months and months of waiting, they got a reply. It said,

"The company has implemented an extensive programme to improve the working conditions, which I hope will reassure members of this group and the 1000 people who signed postcards."

HAYLEY SAYS OF THE CAMPAIGN:

"We can't say our campaign is what they took notice of most, but I do think that our postcards and our campaigning did actually make a difference. With other groups on at them at the same time, they finally collapsed. But it was clear from their letters that they took our campaign seriously."

SO WAS IT WORTH IT?

"It gives you a big feeling of satisfaction doing something like this. We were all terrified of what we were going to get when we went out in public with the trainer. Were we going to be accepted? Were we going to be listened to? As the campaign went on we all got more confident. We wanted to be more involved. We wanted to be out there. To think you've made an impact on all those people's lives working in the factory, it's such a rush - a complete buzz ... definitely worth it."

UNIT 5
COUNCIL AFFAIRS

This unit helps students to

◆ examine various aspects of the work of local government in delivering public services;

◆ consider the issue of fairness in the delivery of public services;

◆ discover some of the remedies open to citizens who feel they have been treated badly.

AT THE COUNCIL

AIMS

◆ To introduce students to some of the functions of local government;

◆ To show how citizens' rights are safeguarded against possible maladministration in local government;

◆ To encourage students to consider just outcomes in situations where citizens have felt aggrieved.

BACKGROUND

This topic uses reports of cases reviewed by the Local Government Ombudsman as a means of clothing the work of local government with some human interest. Each of these cases demonstrates the importance of local government in the lives of citizens. When things go well, these are easily taken for granted. When things go wrong, people's lives can be seriously affected. A further reason for using these reports is that they can help students understand more about the means by which citizens' rights can be upheld in the face of official obstruction or inefficiency. When local governments ignore people's rights, or when they fail to deliver the kind of service citizens are entitled to expect, there must be a remedy. Going to law can be costly and time consuming and is to be avoided if at all possible. The Ombudsman Service for Local Government was set up in 1974 to provide a much easier route to justice.

The Local Government Ombudsman has the power to investigate cases where injustice has occurred through maladministation on the part of local government. In each case the Ombudsman attempts to decide whether: a) there has been an injustice, b) whether any loss was suffered as a result and c) what reparation should be made. As a result of his or her investigations the Ombudsman can also offer guidance on the way local government administration can be improved. Every year the Local Government Ombudsman's office receives and deals with over 15,000 complaints. For the most part, their judgements are not confidential. Annual reports are published every year along with a selection or details of some of the more interesting cases. Material in this topic is drawn from the cases decided in 1997. More up-to-date reports can be obtained, free of charge, from the office of the Commission for Local Adminstration in England, 21 Queen Anne's Gate, London SW1H 9BU. tel: 020 7915 3283.

Ombudsmen have been established to arbitrate in other areas including: banking, building societies, insurance, police, pensions, health service, legal services, and broadcasting.

THE LESSON

Small groups

Divide the class into small groups and give out the Town Hall illustration (page 86) showing different departments of local government. Copy and distribute one or two cases (pages 87 to 89) to each small group. Ask students to look at these real examples in which people have had some kind of trouble which involved the council, pointing out that false names have been used. In each case, ask students to try to decide what has gone wrong and how things should be put right, using the points listed on the sheet.

The Ombudsman's decisions
(sums of money are at 1997 prices)

Craig's special needs
This dispute was about the size of compensation because the council had accepted that it had been in the wrong. The Ombudsman suggested that the compensation paid to Craig's mother should be £2,000.

Case leaves a bad smell
The Ombudsman agreed that the council had not properly enforced its order on the restaurant. The Ombudsman recommended compensation of £500.

Family comes down to earth

The Ombudsman agreed that the council should have been more flexible in considering this case. He felt that the council had taken too long before they finally agreed that the family could be offered somewhere else. He felt that the family had suffered a good deal of stress and inconvenience before the right decision had eventually been made. However, he was not convinced that any great damage had been caused to anyone's health. He recommended that the council should pay the family £1,000 for the unfair treatment, the cost of moving twice and the time and trouble in making the complaint.

Saw point!

The Ombudsman agreed with the Astons that the council had no good reason to go back on the decision it had made earlier. He decided that the policy of placing a wood yard in a residential area had been the wrong one. He ordered the council to compensate the Astons for the drop in the price of their house and to pay them £250 for their trouble in making the complaint.

Nuisance neighbours

The Ombudsman decided that the right action had eventually been taken in issuing the family with the most disruptive children with a notice to quit the house. But if this had been done much earlier, the evidence suggested that a lot of the trouble would have been prevented. The Ombudsman decided the families had suffered a good deal and that they should be paid compensation. This was £800 to Mr and Mrs Rowley and £1,000 to Ms Darby.

TOPIC TWO

PEDESTRIANS ONLY

AIM

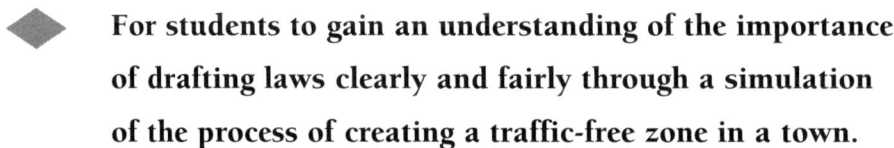

For students to gain an understanding of the importance of drafting laws clearly and fairly through a simulation of the process of creating a traffic-free zone in a town.

BACKGROUND

In the main exercise, students are asked to find a satisfactory form of words following complaints to a council over a plan to ban vehicles from a busy street.

Pedestrianisation schemes of this type are created through powers granted by one of two laws, the **Road Traffic Regulation Act 1990** and the **Town and Country Planning Act 1990**. The choice is likely to depend on the type of pedestrianisation scheme planned by the council. In either case, final approval and the order granting the closure of the street, in England, is likely to rest with the regional Government office.

The final section of the topic provides an opportunity to look at a copy of a real law, and to discuss the importance of clarity in legislation.

The idea of reasonableness

In drafting legislation, the idea of reasonableness is very important and should be firmly grasped by students undertaking this topic. Much of the work of courts also involves determining what is reasonable in relation to a particular set of circumstances. It clearly illustrates the important role of the human element in a system of justice. Justice can never be an impersonally administered process in which inflexible laws are automatically invoked without regard to the people and circumstances involved.

An exemplar Act

The **Intoxicating Substances (Supply) Act 1985** is included to give students an opportunity to handle a piece of Parliamentary legislation. The Act has been chosen because it is:

a) extremely short and comprehensible
b) relevant to young people.

This Act was passed against a background of increasing alarm at the spread of solvent abuse, particularly amongst the age group unable to obtain alcohol. The Act makes it a criminal offence to supply any substance in the knowledge or the reasonable belief that the substance might be inhaled.

The Act attempts to tighten up the laws without actually banning the sale of glues to anyone under 18. This is, therefore, an example of an Act which tries to achieve a reasonable balance between the legitimate needs of those who wish to buy solvents for their proper use and the need to control the sale of solvents to young people who intend to inhale them.

The Act follows a standard format:

a)   The royal coat of arms is always followed by the title of the Act. The year is included to distinguish the Act from others with the same title (eg, there are many 'Education Acts').
b)   The title and description of the Act is followed by the date on which the Act was passed - not to be confused with the date it becomes law (see note (i) below).
c)   The preamble is the same for all Acts.

d) The actual legislation. Notice that Acts have to cover a range of possibilities and therefore have to resort to multiple words and phrases, such as 'supply or offer to supply' and 'knows, or has reasonable cause to believe'. If a word were ambiguous, such as 'supply', it would be the job of the courts to decide on its meaning, in the light of a case or series of cases.

e) It is often possible to claim that particular circumstances altered an action so as to make it not criminal. This is what lawyers call a 'defence'. This Act makes it a defence to prove that the accused person was under 18 at the time of the Act and was not doing it as part of a business. So a 16-year-old offering a substance to a friend would have a defence, but a 16-year-old who was systematically selling to others would be liable to prosecution.

f) The punishment is defined for a criminal offence. 'Summary conviction' means that the offence must be tried in the magistrates' court.

g) Definitions are often included for the sake of clarity. In this case 'controlled drug' is defined in the same way as in another Act. The term includes all those drugs which can only be legally handled by authorised persons.

h) This Act ends with a reference to its title. The title had to be agreed upon in the same way as every other clause in the Act.

i) Acts come into force immediately they receive the royal assent unless there is a delay approved by Parliament. Often the delay is to enable those affected to prepare for it.

j) All Acts have to state clearly which parts of the United Kingdom they will affect.

THE LESSON

1. ### Introduction

Read through THE COUNCIL'S DECISION (page 90) with the students. It gives the background to the exercise. You could ask various members of the class to read the letters of complaint as dramatically as possible. To do this you will need to give your readers some idea of the character they are about to portray - 'a pensioner', 'an angry rate-payer' and so on.

2. ### Small groups

When all the letters have been examined you may want to re-state the problem facing the councillors. They can expand the order, or add footnotes to it, defining the word 'vehicle', or split it into various sub-sections. In groups, let the students wrestle with the problem of deciding on a suitable format for themselves. (This will heighten their appreciation of the format followed by the specimen Act on page 93.)

Allow 20 minutes or so for group work on re-writing the order. This will obviously vary according to the group.

3.   **Class discussion**

When the class is ready, bring them together and discuss each problem in turn. Often there will be general agreement about what to do, in fairness to the people concerned.

Finally, ask each group to read out or display its revised order. As you discuss each solution, try to encourage the students to evaluate the conflicting claims of one group over those of another (eg, the shoppers who want a traffic-free street versus the claims of the shopkeepers for whom this creates some difficulties). Bear in mind that this is more than an exercise in drafting legislation, it is about fairness, or justice and deciding on an appropriate balance between the legitimate desires of several groups. It may be appropriate to introduce the notion of 'lobbying' at this point and of the councillors' need to bear in mind the will of the voters.

AT THE COUNCIL

"THE COUNCIL SHOULD DO SOMETHING ABOUT IT!"

You often hear people talking about the council, but it's not always easy to know what 'the council' does. Roughly speaking, councils run many of our public services such as **education, youth services, libraries, parks and leisure departments** and **social services**. Councils also ensure that roads are repaired and rubbish is collected. When things go right it's easy to forget the council's role in the running of everyday life. Councils are not thought to be very interesting and many people do not bother to vote when it comes to electing councillors. However,

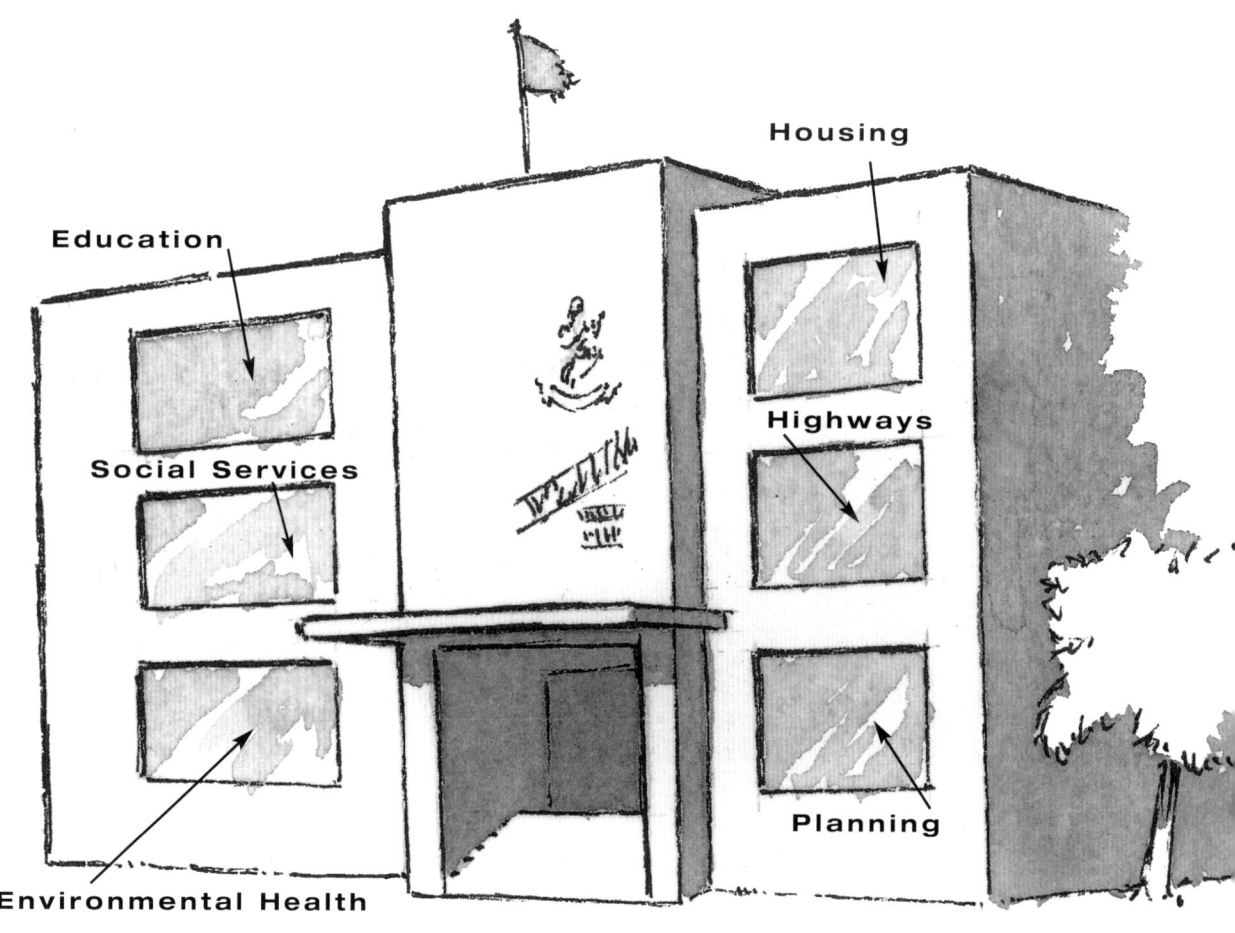

sometimes things happen which makes people realise how much they rely on council services. When things which are the council's responsibility go wrong, people's lives can be seriously affected.

Look at the following real examples in which people have experienced some kind of trouble which involved the council (we have used false names). In each case, try to decide:

◆ which council department each complaint should go to;
◆ what has gone wrong and why;
◆ whether someone has been treated unfairly;
◆ whether someone has lost out in any way;
◆ how should things be put right and whether compensation should be paid. If so, how much?

Your teacher can tell you what happened in each case.

CRAIG'S SPECIAL NEEDS

Craig was a pupil with special needs who became excluded from a primary school because of his bad behaviour. The council took a long time to assess Craig's needs because different departments had to be involved in deciding what was best for him. The case dragged on and in the end Craig lost about four terms of teaching. The council offered his mother some compensation but she thought this was far too little. The cost of a year's schooling at the time (1996) was around £2,000. She complained to the Ombudsman.

HE'S STUDYING GRAVITY.

CASE LEAVES A BAD SMELL

Mr Ahmed lived next door to a very noisy and smelly restaurant, so he complained to the council about it. The environmental health department agreed that the nuisance from the restaurant was very great and told the owner to put things right. However, the owner took no notice and the council were very slow in taking any action. Mr Ahmed complained several times but things got no better. He had to put up with the smell for two and a half years before it was finally sorted out. Mr Ahmed thought this was unreasonable and complained to the Ombudsman.

FAMILY COMES DOWN TO EARTH

When Mr and Mrs Smith and their son became homeless, they asked the council to house them. They each had medical problems which meant that they needed a house or ground floor flat. They provided medical evidence to support their request. However, the council offered them a flat on the fourth floor of a tower block. The family felt this was unsuitable but the council said they had to accept the offer and move in before the council could listen to their appeal. This was normal practice although the council could have made an exception if they had wanted to. The council then took a year before agreeing that the flat was unsuitable for the family after all. During this time the health of the family members had suffered, they had endured a high level of stress and ultimately they had had to pay the cost of moving house twice instead of once.

The Smiths complained to the Ombudsman that they had suffered greatly because of the council's actions.

Saw Point!

Mr and Mrs Aston were horrified to discover that the local council had given planning permission for Mr Blackburn to set up a wood yard next to their house, which was in a quiet country spot. Planning permission for the yard had already been refused once, but when new councillors were elected and Mr Blackburn applied again, the planning committee decided that the business could go ahead. Previously the committee had decided that the yard should go to an area where there were other industries. It should not be allowed in the place where the Astons lived.

As soon as the yard started working, the Astons suffered from the noise it made and their house dropped in value.

They complained to the Ombudsman that they had lost out because the council had made a wrong decision.

Nuisance Neighbours

Mr and Mrs Rowley and Ms Darby were neighbours on a council estate. Some of the local children were making their lives a misery. They made a lot of noise, often playing around a shed in one of the gardens and playing loud music at all hours of the day and evening. They subjected Ms Darby to racial abuse and threw stones and clods of earth into her garden. Once a brick nearly hit Ms Darby's baby. The Rowley and Darby children were afraid to go out. They couldn't go to the shops or play in the park or even in their own gardens. The council contacted the families of the disruptive children but did not issue strict warnings about what could happen if things did not improve. It was only after about two years when one of the families was issued with a notice that their house would be taken away from them, that things did improve.

Mr and Mrs Rowley and Ms Darby complained to the Ombudsman that the council should have dealt more quickly with the behaviour of its tenants.

PEDESTRIANS ONLY

THE COUNCIL'S DECISION

NO VEHICLES ARE ALLOWED IN THE HIGH STREET

BY ORDER

You are a member of a local council. The council has decided to declare the High Street a traffic-free area. This will avoid many traffic jams in this narrow street and will make shopping there more attractive. Almost all the shopkeepers are in favour of the idea as they are sure that it will be good for trade.

The council displays the plans in the main library and asks for the views of the general public. It decides that the order closing the street should be worded as simply as possible, so that everyone can understand it.

Over the next few weeks the council receives a number of letters of complaint. At the next meeting you have to decide whether any alterations should be made.

When you have read all the complaints you will probably feel that the wording of the order should be changed. Rewrite it. Try to be as fair as you can.

Prepare a statement for release to the local papers explaining your reasons for the changes you have made.

8 Rose Avenue
19 September

Dear Sir or Madam,
  Can you clear up an argument? My neighbour insists that the plans to keep vehicles out of the High Street apply to kiddies' bikes as well.
  Surely that's not right. What are they supposed to do? Wait at the end of the street until the parents have finished shopping?
  Can you make the wording of the plans clearer, please?

Yours,

Eileen O'Leary (Mrs)

Cherry House, 7 Wood Street
10 October

Dear Sir,
  If your plans go through to stop cars in the High Street you'll make it a paradise for kids with skateboards and bikes.
  In any case aren't skateboards and bikes banned as well? Surely, they are vehicles?
  Yours faithfully,

Sharmila Manglani

HELP THE INFIRM

15 September

To the Town Clerk,

Dear Sir,
  Recently, we have had a number of enquiries from users of wheelchairs and cars specially adapted for disabled drivers, concerning the effects of banning vehicles in the High Street.
  If the plans really mean no vehicles at all in the street then we feel you will be discriminating against the disabled in a quite unfair way. Will 'vehicle' apply to cars driven by the disabled, or powered wheelchairs, or hand-driven wheelchairs or all three?
  Could not all three types of vehicles be allowed?
  The council has shown itself sympathetic to the needs of the disabled in the past. They have the right to lead as full a life as possible and we feel this includes proper access to all the town's public buildings including the main shops in the High Street.
  Thanking you for your consideration.

Yours faithfully,

Margaret Goldberg (Mrs)
President

County Hall
Fire Department
7th September

Dear Sir,

Proposal to close the High Street to vehicles

Report to Chief Fire Officer

Two days ago my officers carried out a thorough survey of the High Street area to look for possible problems if the plans to close the street are carried out.

The access to the rear of the shops is through Castle Street. This is narrow even when empty and, during working hours, it is usually parked along both sides. Access would certainly be slower using this route.

If the High Street is closed, I must request that it should still be possible for fire engines to reach the fronts of all shops. Seats, potted shrubs and so on must be arranged so that quick access is still possible.

I am sure that you will receive similar requests from the ambulance service and the police.

Yours faithfully,

P.S. Stott
Chief Fire Officer

---

1 Hillcroft Crescent

1 November

Sir or Madam,
  On behalf of taxpayers and car-owners of this town, I wish to state my objections to the proposed blockading of the High Street against cars. If I want to go into town for a few odds and ends, it will take me hours looking for somewhere to park. What was wrong with the old system of allowing us to park for 20 minutes right outside the shops?
  After all, what do we pay our council tax for, if not to keep the roads in good condition so that we can use them? Who wants potted trees all down the High Street? The council should ask itself where it would be without those of us who own cars.

Yours very sincerely,

Anthony Ashe

To the Council,

Dear Sirs,
  As the owner of Kash and Karry Ltd., I would like to protest most strongly about the effect on my business of the plans to close the High Street. This will mean that my suppliers will refuse to deliver to me as their lorries have to park at the end of the street.
  The drivers are refusing to bring goods right to the shop as this involves many trips with a hand truck and they say it's not their job. If you can't do something about this, I shall go out of business and I'm not the only one. I am taking legal advice as to whether I could sue for loss of earnings.

Yours sincerely,

A McKee.

IN THE ACT

Read the text of the **Intoxicating Substances (Supply) Act 1985**, one of the shorter Acts of that year!

This Act was passed when MPs became aware of the fact that many young people, who were too young to buy alcohol, were buying glue from hardware shops to sniff. Some shopkeepers, it seemed, were also selling plastic bags as a sniffing 'kit'.

Notice that the Act makes it an offence to sell glue knowing it will be abused. It has to allow for glue still to be bought for proper use. A good deal of the debates amongst councillors and MPs focus on getting the wording of the law right – badly worded Acts can make life very difficult for people. Each new law also has to be enforceable, otherwise it will not be followed.

Study the Act, and try to identify these features which can be found in all Acts of Parliament:

❶ the general description of the Act, and the date on which it was passed

❷ the declaration that the Act has been passed by the Houses of Parliament and has the Queen's official approval

❸ the main body of the Act, containing the new laws

❹ the punishment that can be given to a person found guilty of breaking the new law

❺ the scope of the Act (each Act states which of the countries in the United Kingdom are affected) and the date on which it came into force.

If you could be Prime Minister for a short time, what one law would you introduce?

INTOXICATING SUBSTANCES (SUPPLY) ACT 1985

1985 CHAPTER 26

An Act to prohibit the supply to persons under the age of eighteen of certain substances which may cause intoxication if inhaled.

[13th June 1985]

BE IT ENACTED by the Queen's most Excellent Majesty, by and with the advice and consent of the Lords Spiritual and Temporal, and Commons, in this present Parliament assembled, and by the authority of the same, as follows:–

1.– (1) It is an offence for a person to supply or offer to supply a substance other than a controlled drug–

    (a) to a person under the age of eighteen whom he knows, or has reasonable cause to believe, to be under that age;

or

    (b) to a person–

        (i) who is acting on behalf of a person under that age; and

        (ii) whom he knows, or has reasonable cause to believe, to be so acting,

if he knows or has reasonable cause to believe that the substance is, or its fumes are, likely to be inhaled by the person under the age of eighteen for the purpose of causing intoxication.

Offence of supply of intoxicating substance

(2) In proceedings against any person for an offence under subsection (1) above it is a defence for him to show that at the time he made the supply or offer he was under the age of eighteen and was acting otherwise than in the course or furtherance of a business.

(3) A person guilty of an offence under this section shall be liable on summary conviction to imprisonment for a term not exceeding six months or to a fine not exceeding level 5 on the standard scale (as defined in section 75 of the Criminal Justice Act 1982), or to both.

1982 c.48.

(4) In this section "controlled drug" has the same meaning as in the Misuse of Drugs Act 1971.

1971 c.38.

2.– (1) This Act may be cited as the Intoxicating Substances (Supply) Act 1985.

Short title, commencement and extent

(2) This Act shall come into force at the end of the period of two months beginning with the day on which it is passed.

(3) This Act extends to Northern Ireland but not to Scotland.

UNIT 6

CHANGING FOR THE BETTER

This unit helps students to

◆ examine how new laws are made and how existing laws are changed or updated;

◆ understand that a wide range of issues debated in Parliament are relevant to young people.

TOPIC ONE

A PROBLEM FOR CYCLISTS

AIMS

◆ To examine some of the practical and legal difficulties facing young people cycling on busy or dangerous roads;

◆ To consider how cycling could be made safer, including whether changes in the law would help.

BACKGROUND

A picture story is used to ask whether there should be changes in the law to make cycling safer.

The number of pedal cyclists killed in Britain each year has fallen steadily since the end of World War Two. In 1990 there were 256 fatalities, and in 1998 there were 158, compared with 918 in 1945. Current UK statistics for pedal cyclist deaths per head of population are also low compared with the rest of Europe. Only Finland and Spain have fewer deaths than the United Kingdom, per head of population. The country with the most fatalities is the Netherlands.

A major cause of the reduction in deaths of pedal cyclists has been a sharp decline in recent years in the use of bicycles on the road. For example, far fewer children cycle to school today than twenty years ago. Data published by the Commission of the European Communities indicates that four per cent of journeys in the UK are by pedal cycle, compared with 11 per cent in Germany, 16 per cent in Sweden and 18 per cent in Denmark. In some Dutch cities, bicycles are used for 40 to 50 per cent of all journeys. Therefore when the use of the pedal cycle is taken into account, casualty rates in Britain become higher than in some other European countries.

Riding a pedal cycle on a footpath remains an offence under Section 72 of the **Highways Act 1835**. There is no mention of bicycles by name in this law, passed four years before the invention of the self-propelled bicycle. There is instead a general reference to any person who wilfully rides 'on a footpath by the side of a road or set apart for the use or accommodation of foot passengers'.

This is an area of law which has tended to fall into disregard by virtue of the changed situation on the roads. Contrary to popular opinion, it is against the law for even a child to ride a bicycle (or tricycle) on the pavement, but there is clearly a lack of public will in most situations to drive young cyclists off the pavement on to the road. RoSPA (the Royal Society for the Prevention of Accidents) would support a change in its law to allow young children not capable of riding on the roads safely to ride on footpaths.

The legal position of scooters, a craze which began in the 1990s, is unclear according to the RoSPA. They recommend users should not ride them on the road, but it may be illegal to ride them on pavements, strictly speaking. At any rate, care should be taken: in 1998 over 2,000 people went to hospital with scooter-related injuries, and that was before the craze took off.

THE LESSON

1.   **A picture story**

Read the picture story on page 99 with the class and invite reactions to the dilemma facing Anna about how to cross the busy main road. Should she ride her bicycle on the pavement as her mother says? What would the class do in her position? How many students regularly ride their bike on the pavement? Should the police take action in such cases? If not, then perhaps it is time to change the law – but if so, how would students change it?

2. **Class discussion**

Read the letters on page 100, which take the exercise a stage further. Ask the students to give their answers to the questions on the page, and discuss their responses.

3. **Small groups**

The information on page 101, **TOUGH NUTS**, gives details of accidents involving cyclists. Ask students, in pairs or groups, to draw up a list of ways in which the number of accidents to cyclists could be reduced. Encourage students to think of measures affecting both cyclists and motorists. Ask them to rank their ideas, and then to write - perhaps for display - a more detailed proposal on their best suggestion. Students who find difficulty in writing at length on one proposal may find it easier to write a couple of sentences about their first three ideas.

4. **Extension activity**

If there is time, the question of the safety of cyclists in the vicinity of the school can also be considered. Ask students to trace their route to school on a map and discuss the danger spots for those who cycle to school. If any accident black spots emerge, students might consider what might be done to reduce the likelihood of further accidents. Use the internet to research accident statistics for cyclists.

This could include writing to local councillors about their ideas for improvements, and inviting a local politician, police officer, or road safety officer into school to discuss the problem further.

TOPIC TWO

HELMET HEADACHES

AIMS

◆ To discuss the arguments for and against the compulsory wearing of cycle safety helmets;

◆ To introduce the basic elements of a parliamentary debate.

BACKGROUND

This topic is in two parts. In the first, pupils discuss the advantages and disadvantages of legislation making the wearing of crash helmets compulsory for cyclists. If time allows, they can move on to the second part and draft and debate a Bill designed to enforce the wearing of cycle safety helmets.

Although ministers have powers to pass regulations vested in them by statute, fundamental changes in the law can only be made by Parliament. Proposals for a new law are introduced into the House of Commons or House of Lords in the form of a Bill. Most Bills first appear in the Commons. At the **first reading**, the title of the Bill is announced to MPs, and a date is set for the second reading.

At the **second reading**, the principles of the Bill are debated by Parliament. If these are rejected, the Bill proceeds no further.

If accepted, the Bill moves to the **committee stage**, where a group of MPs, chosen on the basis of party strength and specialist qualification, examines and possibly amends the Bill, clause by clause.

The amended Bill is brought back to the main body of the House for the **report stage**, where amendments are debated. If approved, the Bill is given its third reading, and is passed to the House of Lords, where it follows a series of stages similar to those in the Commons. The House of Lords may amend the Bill, but all amendments must be approved by the House of Commons.

The Bill is then given the royal assent and becomes law. The monarch no longer actually signs Bills. The monarch's assent today is just a constitutional convention.

THE LESSON

1.   Class discussion

Give out page 102. Ask the class to think of reasons why cyclists may be for or against wearing safety helmets. This discussion is likely to raise questions of peer group pressure and the need felt by many people to maintain a certain image.

2.   An opinion poll

Carry out a poll into the numbers of students in the class who wear a helmet and their attitudes towards wearing them. If time is available, this can take the form of a more detailed questionnaire.

Collect the results of this opinion poll and discuss the significant points. For example, how many appear to be influenced by the opinions and behaviour of their friends? What are the difficulties of starting a trend, or of being the odd one out?

3. **Small groups**

Read **SHOULD THE LAW BE CHANGED?** (page 103). Ask students to list the arguments for and against making the wearing of cycle helmets compulsory.

If the majority of the class is in favour of changing the law, pupils can use the Bill on page 104 and the information on page 105 to gain some idea of the parliamentary procedure surrounding the creation of new laws.

4. **Class debate**

Discussion of the Bill, clause by clause, will help students understand the complexities of the issue and the difficulties facing those who wish to bring about social change. Clauses may be added or amended according to the ideas coming from the class. Remind the class that the law has to be carefully worded and great consideration given to matters such as who should be excluded from its provisions.

Although the number of MPs on the committees which scrutinise a Bill is often large (between 20 and 60), this stage is most easily managed in class with students in small groups of no more than six. Give students a copy of page 105 and use this to explain, in general terms, how laws are made or changed by Parliament.

Provide pupils with a copy of the imaginary **Safety Helmet (Cyclists) Bill**, page 104. Ask them to look at each clause and decide whether it should be changed before the Bill becomes law. According to the age and ability of the class, you may also wish to look at the difficulties of defining terms - a problem always faced by those who make rules or laws. This can be an interesting exercise in itself and can help develop important language skills. What is meant by 'helmet' (is a turban to count?), 'road', and 'cycling'? It must be made clear what should and should not be included under these terms.

The term 'cycle' may also need defining. Is 'cycle' to refer only to two-wheeled vehicles and should scooters and skateboards be included? Should it include three-wheeled vehicles, or perhaps only those tricycles ridden by adults? For the purposes of this Bill, children's bicycles fitted with stabilisers might be excluded from the meaning of the word.

Each group should produce a copy of their completed Bill for display. Use these to indicate to the whole class the kind of amendments that were made.

RESOURCES

Teaching materials and statistics on all aspects of road safety are published by the Royal Society for the Prevention of Accidents (RoSPA) RoSPA House, Edgbaston Park, 353 Bristol Road, Birmingham B5 7ST, 0121 248 2000 www.rospa.org.uk

A PROBLEM FOR CYCLISTS

Which Way?

Was Anna's mum right to tell her to ride on the pavement?
Was Anna right to have ridden on the road?

A police officer on duty sees two young people aged 12 and 14 cycling on
the pavement. This is against the law. What should the police officer do?

WHAT THE LAW SAYS

Under the **Highways Act 1835**, it is against the law for anyone to ride
on a footpath or pavement.
A person found to have broken this law can be fined up to £500,
although the actual fine will depend on how well off the offender is.

PAVING THE WAY

Should the law be changed? Here are three points of view based on real letters to a newspaper ...

◆ With whom do you sympathise the most?
◆ What would you say to the writer of the first letter who says he will break the law?
◆ Should the law be changed to allow cycling on the pavement?
◆ What would be the best wording of a law which made it legal for cyclists to ride on pavements?
◆ What alternative suggestions can you make which will improve road safety for cyclists?

Dear Sir,

The roads near my home are very busy, and I sometimes ride my bike on the pavement to escape the dangers of the traffic. One day, while riding on the pavement on my way back from work, I was stopped by a police officer and told that I must either walk with my bike, or ride it in the road.

I finished my journey on foot – but I will not do the same again. If the police decide to prosecute me I hope they will do the same to all motorists who either drive or park their cars on the pavements?

Dennis Adams
Manchester

Dear Sir,

I think Dennis Adams is right.

People should be allowed to cycle on the footpath if they wish, as long as they do not put pedestrians in any danger.

Why not make a speed limit of five miles per hour for this?

Tracey Farmer
Barnsley

Dear Sir,

I hope Dennis Adams is arrested by a police officer next time he rides his bike on the pavement.

Life is already difficult enough for the pedestrian with such hazards as parked cars, overhanging branches and all the mess that dog owners allow their animals to leave behind. Don't add to our problems by letting cyclists loose on the pavement as well.

Alice Bottomley
London

TOUGH NUTS

CYCLING ACCIDENTS - FACTS AND FIGURES

In 1998 there were nearly 23,000 cyclists injured in accidents. About one third of these were children. About 70 per cent of cyclists killed or seriously injured received major head injuries, including fractured skulls and brain damage.

PEDAL CYCLISTS KILLED, BY AGE AND GENDER (1998)

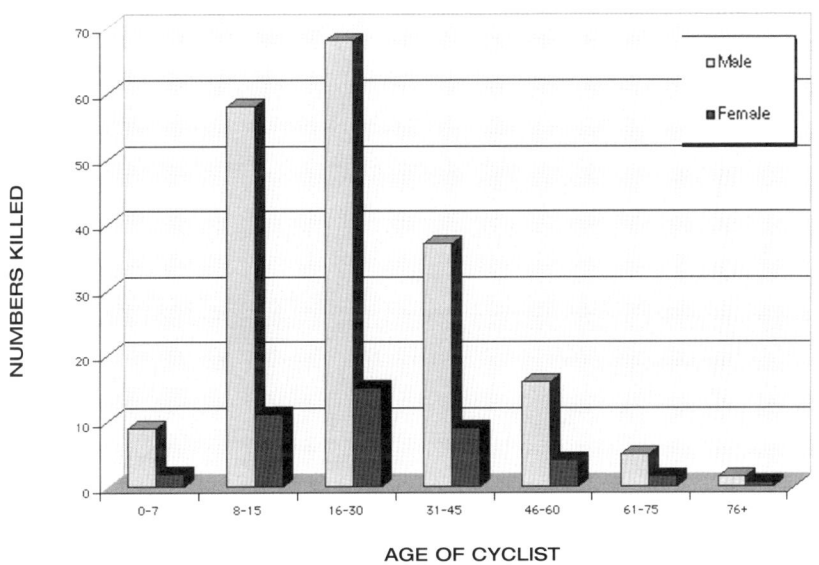

WHO IS TO BLAME FOR ACCIDENTS?

When accidents occur involving cyclists and motor vehicles, it is thought that the motorist is at fault in about 65 per cent of cases.

The cyclist is thought to be at fault in about 25 per cent of cases.

Both the motorist and the cyclist are thought to be at fault in about 10 per cent of cases.

Use the information on this page to help you draw up a list of ways cycling could be made safer. Put these in order, with your best idea for safer cycling coming first.

HELMET HEADACHES

'ONE DAY I'LL GET ONE…'

WHY DO SOME PEOPLE WEAR A HELMET, AND OTHERS NOT?

Make up a short questionnaire to find out what people think about wearing cycle helmets. You could include questions on …

◆ the number of people who regularly wear a helmet when cycling;
◆ why some people do not wear a safety helmet;
◆ whether people would feel safer wearing a helmet;
◆ whether more people would wear a helmet if their friends did so;
◆ whether there is a difference between what young people and adults think about this;
◆ whether the cost of buying a helmet is preventing some people from wearing one.

SHOULD THE LAW BE CHANGED?

If all cyclists wore safety helmets, there would be fewer deaths and serious injuries and money would be saved on hospital bills.

Some people feel that passing a law to make cycle helmets compulsory is the best way to reduce head injuries. They say that lessons can be learnt from what happened when helmets for motorcyclists were made compulsory. Many people thought that motorcyclists should be free to decide for themselves whether to wear a helmet. Eventually a law was passed in 1972 making it compulsory for them to wear a crash helmet. Many deaths and serious injuries have been prevented as a result.

Wearing a helmet does not prevent a cyclist from having an accident. A cyclist may still be badly hurt even if he or she is wearing a helmet. The helmets are only designed to give protection from a fall, not from a collision with a moving vehicle.

Make a list of reasons in favour of using the law to force cyclists to wear crash helmets. Make a list of reasons against making cycle helmets compulsory.

Look at the Safety Helmets (Cyclists) Bill and debate it as if you were in Parliament. Propose changes to the wording to improve the Bill, such as lowering the age limit or raising the fine.

Safety Helmets (Cyclists) Bill

A Bill

An Act to make compulsory the wearing of safety helmets for cyclists.

B E IT ENACTED by the Queen's most Excellent Majesty, by and with the advice and consent of the Lords Spiritual and Temporal, and Commons, in this present Parliament assembled, and by the authority of the same, as follows:-

1.   It shall be an offence for cyclists not to wear a safety helmet whilst cycling on the roads.

2.   It shall be an offence for the parent of a child under ten years of age to allow him or her to cycle on the road without a safety helmet.

3.   A person guilty of an offence under this Act shall be liable to a fine of up to £100.

4.   This law shall come into force one year after receiving the royal assent.

CHANGING THE LAW

One of the jobs of a Member of Parliament (MP) is to play a part in making and changing the law. It usually takes a long time to change the law, because a new law - or Bill as it is known - is discussed and debated several times by MPs before it becomes law.

This is what usually happens ...

FIRST READING

◆ Just the title of the Bill is read out in Parliament. The Bill is printed and a date is fixed for its next reading.

SECOND READING

◆ The main ideas behind the Bill are discussed by MPs in Parliament, and then voted on. If MPs agree with the Bill, it passes to the next stage. If not, the Bill is not discussed any more and cannot become law.

COMMITTEE STAGE

◆ A committee of MPs discusses the Bill in great detail. This is where sections of the Bill might be changed.

REPORT STAGE

◆ The Bill, as changed by the committee of MPs, comes back to the 'whole house' (all MPs) to be approved. Changes are still possible at this stage.

THIRD READING

◆ The Bill is debated again as a whole, and voted on.

HOUSE OF LORDS

◆ When the Bill has gone through all these stages, it is passed to the House of Lords where it is debated in a similar way.

◆ The House of Lords is made up of senior politicians who have been made members of the Lords, senior bishops, senior judges and some members of the aristocracy with inherited titles.

◆ Any changes to the Bill made by the House of Lords have to be approved by the House of Commons before they can become law.

◆ MPs in the House of Commons will take note of the ways in which the House of Lords thinks that the Bill should be changed - but they don't have to follow them.

THE ROYAL ASSENT

◆ When the Bill has been agreed by both Houses of Parliament it is given the 'royal assent' (approval) and becomes an Act of Parliament.

UNIT 7

HERE IS THE NEWS

This unit helps students to

◆ examine the role of the media in a free society;

◆ critically review how the news is reported.

TRUE OR FALSE?

AIM

◆ To encourage students to take a critical view of the question of bias and objectivity in newspaper reporting.

BACKGROUND

Students gain their knowledge of the social world from a number of sources, including parents, friends, television and newspapers. One recent survey found that newspapers were the least trusted as souces of reliable information. This topic examines the issue of bias in reporting and asks whether any reporting can ever be completely objective.

THE LESSON

1. A newspaper article

Copy and distribute the newspaper article on teenage drinking (pages 111 to 112). Ask students to consider the questions on page 112 and analyse the content of the article from the point of view of the different positions put forward within it, asking whether each side has put its case well. Point out that the Institute of Alcohol Studies which wrote the report on which the article is based is funded by the anti-alcohol lobby. Who is to be believed and why? Introduce the concepts of 'vested interests' and 'pressure group' if you feel this is appropriate. Is the report itself put together fairly?

2. **Written work**

Ask students to write an article in the style of a tabloid newspaper in which they use persuasive writing to campaign for something they would like to see changed.

FOR TRUTH AND JUSTICE

AIM

◆ **To examine the ways in which newspapers can act as champions of citizens' interests.**

BACKGROUND

In this topic, students reflect on two real cases where newspapers have uncovered scandals of different kinds.

THE LESSON

1. **Class discussion**

Read and discuss pages 113 and 114, which give two examples of the way in which newspapers can act as champions of citizens' interests, exposing poor standards in public life or scandals which otherwise might not come to light. Point out that sometimes people will give the papers information because of the established practice that journalists never reveal their sources. In some instances this allows them to work in ways the police cannot.

Ask students how far they agree with people who say that the papers should not print stories about people's private lives. Discuss what happens when the papers print stories about famous people which the celebrities claim are not true. Relate this discussion to the right to privacy and respect for one's family life, as included in the **Human Rights Act 1998**.

2. Further activities

● As a class put together the front page of a class (or school) newspaper. Ask students to think about what kind of stories would be most interesting for their readers and how should they be written.

● Give out a selection of local and national newspapers to each group and ask students to compare them. How good are the local papers at telling people about what is going on in the community?

● Ask students to imagine that a national company is launching a paper for their age group. What would they advise the company to include in the paper to make it as attractive as possible?

TOPIC THREE

TELLING IT LIKE IT IS?

AIM

◆ **To encourage a critical understanding of the role newspapers play in bringing the news to their readers and the function they fulfil in democratic life.**

BACKGROUND

This topic asks students to compare a number of papers and draw conclusions about their aims, target audience, and so on.

For this exercise you will need to ask students to bring in a range of newspapers from home, bearing in mind that some papers carry material which some pupils and parents would consider offensive. Alternatively, select and copy articles from different papers covering the same story and invite the class to compare and contrast.

THE LESSON

1.   **Small groups**

Give each group at least one tabloid newspaper and one broadsheet for comparison. Ask students to make a list of the different features, such as crosswords or TV listings, they can find. What percentage of the paper is actually news? (This can vary quite a lot between papers.) What are the news items about (eg, are they about politics and current affairs or something else)?

It is often said that you cannot believe everything you read in the papers. How true do the students think this might be? Ask them to think of some reasons why the stories in the newspapers they are looking at may not be completely accurate.

2.   **Class discussion**

Even though TV and radio bring us the news much more immediately than a paper can, newspapers are still very popular. Why do the students think this is?

3.   **Small groups**

Ask students to identify and compare the same story as published in two or three different papers. (Ensure that each group considers at least one tabloid and one broadsheet newspaper.) Ask them to study the facts as they occur in each article. Do they think the papers disagree over the facts of the story in any way? Are the stories different in any other sense? For example, does one paper leave out some details that others include? Explain that this is one way in which papers can put a bias on the stories they carry. Sometimes they place the stories in different parts of the paper. What differences can students find between their papers on this point?

Explain that these are the kinds of difference between papers which can give us a clue as to what political viewpoint the paper supports. Sometimes this shows very clearly in the headline the paper puts above the story. A headline does not always give a very good description of the story that follows it. Ask students to consider how accurate the headlines are in the papers they are studying; are there differences in style between the papers?

4. **Class discussion**

As a class, discuss the question 'Are there any papers which simply tell the truth, and nothing but the truth?' Do the students think it is possible to be completely unbiased about social events or problems? Some papers are biased towards a particular political party. Could the students tell from the papers they read, which parties they might support? Does this mean that papers which don't support any parties are unbiased and more reliable? Probably not, is the answer. All newspapers have to make money and therefore they each have to appeal to a certain type of reader. This means that papers need to include the type of news, articles, features, letters and so on which that kind of reader wants to read. This makes every newspaper biased in some way, though students may decide, after looking at them, that some papers try to tell their readers what to think more than others do.

5. **Homework**

It is interesting to compare newspaper bias with what happens with TV and radio bulletins. By law, these have to be as fair as possible in their coverage of politics. Why do students think this is? But even here, every news programme is keen to offer the kind of stories it thinks its own type of viewer wants to see. Otherwise they switch over or switch off.

For homework, ask students to plot the news stories covered on children's TV news bulletins and compare these with the stories covered on the adult news over a period of a week. What differences can they find? How good do they think the children's news programmes are? Should there be more or less news coverage for young people on TV?

6. **A survey**

Ask students to conduct (or take part in) a survey of young people's newspaper reading habits. This could be either across the school or within the class. Which papers are read, how often and by whom? Data from different classes could be used to build up a wider picture. For homework, students could also ask a small sample of adults about what papers they read and why.

TRUE OR FALSE?

Read the following article. Can you tell which are factual statements and which are opinions in the following story? If there is a bias, does the bias come from the newspaper reporter or somewhere else?

The article is closely based on one which appeared in a national tabloid newspaper in March 2001.

SCANDAL AS DRINK BOSSES TARGET OUR KIDS

A REPORT OUT today accuses Britain's drinks industry of targeting children as young as 11 to boost their profits. Health experts attacked drinks bosses for their 'greed' in trying to win over the young. They hit out at advertising which tries to lure young people on to alcohol through promotions, sports sponsorship and alcopop-style drinks.

The report by the Institute of Alcohol Studies, which is against the abuse of alcohol, warns that getting children hooked on drink will cripple the NHS, increase crime levels and create more social problems.

The report suggests that children are bombarded with positive images of alcohol drinking, including football strips for small children with drinks logos all over them. As a result young people are drinking at an earlier age, drinking more often and greater quantities. Some people have claimed that the drinks industry seemed to want to trap people early as the tobacco trade had done for years.

continued over...

BRITAIN TOP OF THE LEAGUE

Recent studies reveal that Britain is near the top of the league in Europe for teenage drink abuse leading to rising levels of pregnancy, truancy, violence and theft. 33 per cent of boys and 27 per cent of girls had been drunk when they were 13 or under. In England, 14 per cent of 11 year-old boys and nine per cent of girls admit to drinking beer, wine or spirits once a week or more.

Earlier this week an inquest heard how a 16 year-old boy from Norwich drowned shortly after being turned away from a nightclub because he was drunk. The Coroner said there was a 'vast amount' of alcohol in the teenager's system when his body was found in the River Wensum.

Experts warn that the problem of heavy drinking among UK youngsters coincided with the launch of alcopops in 1995.

Drink-related illness costs the NHS £6 billion every year – 12 per cent of its total budget.

However, the Portman Group, which represents the drinks industry, said the report was misleading and inaccurate. A spokesman said that self-regulation of advertising was working and if the authors of the report had any serious concerns in this area they should make a formal complaint rather than make unfounded claims.

What are the problems in finding out the truth from this piece?

◆ What sources has the reporter used to put the story together?
◆ How did the reporter make the story more dramatic? What does the story about the boy who drowned prove?
◆ How well did the spokesman for the drinks industry answer the complaints?
◆ What evidence is offered that 'alcopops' are partly to blame?

FOR TRUTH AND JUSTICE

You might think that it would be good idea to pass a law saying that the papers should not report anything that was untrue - so that the public could always rely on what they were reading. In some countries papers can only print what the government allows them to. But is that the same thing? Who would decide what 'truth' the public were allowed to know?

In fact, tough censorship laws can be very dangerous to democracy because governments can more easily feed the public their side of the story - this is called propaganda. This is why many people say we need a 'free press' in democratic societies. One of the things newspapers often do well is to uncover stories that governments want to keep quiet for some reason.

Read this example of how newspapers kept a watch on the government over a public health issue.

DID THE GOVERNMENT FAILURE RISK LIVES?

In 1995 a report warned the government about the dangers of unclean abattoirs. It said that poor hygiene in our slaughter houses meant there was a clear risk of spreading the dangerous E-coli bug. Then two years later, a serious outbreak in Scotland killed at least 20 people. When reporters were told about the report which had been gathering dust, they began to ask awkward questions. It turned out that the government had not acted on the report and had told almost no one about it. It appears that the government had not wanted to add to the meat industry's problems because it was already in serious trouble over the spread of BSE, the brain disease.

When the newspapers ran the story, MPs and many others were furious. If standards had been higher the E-coli outbreak might never have happened.

The Minister of Agriculture was forced to make a statement in Parliament. He claimed that although the report had not been properly published it had been made available to everyone who needed to know about it. However, reporters found out that

113

this was not completely true. To protect the farming industry, it looks as if the Ministry of Agriculture had not told the public something it had a right to know. Many people believed that the government had made a mistake and was trying to 'cover up'. The newspapers had told the public the truth.

FOUL PLAY

Here is another example of how the papers can expose a scandal.

In August 1994, *The Sun* received a tip-off that Bruce Grobbelaar, the Liverpool goalkeeper, had accepted bribes to fix matches. The paper decided to try to catch him out and invented a story about a foreign betting group that would be willing to pay Grobbelaar for the right results in Liverpool's games.

The man who had tipped off *The Sun* was a friend of Grobbelaar's. He was given secret recording equipment and sent by the paper to encourage Grobbelaar to do a deal. The paper used hidden cameras to record the moment when Grobbelaar took £2,000 to do what the betting group wanted.

When *The Sun* ran the story Grobbelaar sued for libel, claiming the story was a lie. He won his case and was awarded £85,000 to make up for the damage to his reputation. *The Sun* was criticised for the way it had got the story because it had tricked Grobbelaar and encouraged him to break the law. However, the paper stuck by its story and appealed to a higher court. The appeal court decided that the first verdict had been a wrong one and that Grobbelaar was guilty after all.

UNIT 8

BE HEALTHY, BE SAFE

This unit helps students to

◆ consider the role of the law in regulating legal and illegal drugs in society;

◆ examine the law surrounding young people and part-time work, and consider why the law is involved in this area of life.

THE GRIM DEATH TOLL FROM SMOKING

AIMS

◆ To examine the role of law in regulating smoking;

◆ To examine the difficult question of whether it is ever right to compel individuals to act against their will, even when it is probably in their best interests to do so;

◆ To encourage understanding of an aspect of public policy.

BACKGROUND

The example of smoking has been used to illustrate the conflict between improving health and restricting liberty. It may be appropriate to draw parallels between this and other issues, such as the controversies which surround the passing of various road traffic laws - speed limits, seat belts and breathalysers. In 1853, the vaccination of children against smallpox was made compulsory by law. It faced much public opposition - demonstrations were held in many towns and cities throughout Britain, and parents were fined and even imprisoned for refusing to comply. Gladstone, in 1871, called vaccination 'an attack on private liberty', and Robert Peel termed it 'contrary to the mental habits of the British'.

After completing this topic, students should understand:
- that there are limitations to the law, and that governments are often unwilling to create laws which lack the support of a significant part of the population;
- the need to balance the interests of the community against the freedoms of the individual.

THE LESSON

1. A newspaper article

Read the newspaper article (page 121) with the class. Ask students to consider whether smoking should be banned or limited in some way through, say, restrictions on smoking in public places. Take a preliminary poll of opinion in the class, then present information on the health effects of smoking. Debate the issue and then take a second poll to see how much opinion has changed.

2. Class discussion

Read the paragraph under the heading **FREEDOM TO THE END!** (page 123) with the class and consider the facts on **YOUNG PEOPLE AND SMOKING** (page 122). Ask students to imagine they are members of a government commission set up to draft harsh new anti-smoking laws. Discuss the issues raised under the heading **TALKING POINTS** (page 123). The exercise is designed to raise issues concerning the practicalities of outlawing a practice against the wishes of a significant proportion of the population. This may help students to understand why it is difficult to legislate against practices such as smoking, which are generally agreed to be harmful. A vital lesson concerning law is that a law may not be viable if it does not have the consent of a significant proportion of the population.

GOOD HEALTH!

AIMS

◆ To present students with a variety of facts relating to the use of alcohol and its effects;

◆ To ask students to take on different roles and select facts to develop a particular case.

BACKGROUND

Against a background of rapidly changing social attitudes towards alcohol consumption, especially amongst young people, students consider the need for greater regulation to prevent a number of personal and social consequences.

THE LESSON

1. **Class discussion**

Read THE EFFECTS OF ALCOHOL (page 124) with the class. Ask students to indicate whether they have any feelings of their own about the seriousness of the problem and which they consider the main issues to be. You could use the section on drink-driving (page 125) separately or link it with this exercise.

2. **Small groups**

Read MAKING CHOICES (page 128) and ask students to consider whether they themselves would favour adopting any of the measures suggested. Allow the class to discuss the options in twos or threes, but suggest that the options they choose should be their own despite what other members of the group feel. Ask them if they feel the law should be changed and if so, in what way.

3. **Pairs**

Read ARGUING A CASE (page 129) with the class. In this exercise students are asked to develop a set of arguments in favour of a point of view which they may not share. The value of the exercise is to understand how to present a case by emphasising certain key points at the expense of others. Other strategies might be to appeal to the emotions of people's self-interest if necessary. Such an exercise will increase their awareness of how the same facts can be used to support a range of viewpoints.

Allocate a role card number to each pair. Ask pupils, in pairs, to use the evidence on pages 124 to 127 to present the case suggested in the form of a letter.

4. Class discussion

After the exercise, consider with the students how they tackled the problem with regard to the use of statistics or facts. Which arguments did they decide to emphasise and which to ignore or play down? Some members of the class could be asked to read out their letters and the techniques they adopted could be discussed and analysed.

WORK AND PLAY

AIM

◆ **To acquaint students with the law relating to young people's part-time employment, and to provide them with the opportunity to think critically about some issues relating to child labour.**

BACKGROUND

Since earliest times, children working with their parents have contributed to the family economy. The change to a factory-based economy in the eighteenth and nineteenth centuries brought about a dramatic shift in this relationship, as the workplace of many children moved out of the home. Factory owners and politicians were slow to acknowledge the abuse of children that persisted at this time. Through economic necessity, children worked for long hours in factories under appalling conditions. Pay was abysmal, and injuries and even deaths at work were not uncommon.

Through the efforts of reformers such as Richard Oastler, Michael Sadier and Lord Shaftesbury, the **Factories Regulation Act 1833** was passed, forbidding the employment of children below the age of nine in the textile industry and limiting hours of work in other industries. For the first time a small inspectorate was also established. Previous Acts of this sort had had no means of enforcement.

In 1840, a Royal Commission was set up to investigate employment of children in the mines. Inspectors for the Commission found conditions there even worse than in the mills. Details of reports from a number of mines have been combined in **THE WAY WE WERE** (page 130). Soon after the Commission published its findings, the **Mines and Colleries Act 1842** was passed, though not without difficulty. The Act stated that children below the age of 10 could not work underground and an inspectorate was established for its implementation. The Act did not limit the hours that children over 10 could work nor did it introduce any new safety regulations. The young people quoted, therefore, probably derived little benefit from this law.

The employment of children was further controlled by the **Education Acts 1870 and 1880**. The latter made school compulsory for all children up to the age of 10. Other changes followed with the **Pedlars Certificates Act 1871**, which made it an offence for children under 17 to go from door to door selling most things other than vegetables and fruit, and the **Factory and Workshops Act 1878**, which applied the terms of the 1842 Act to all industries.

The current legislation is derived from the **Employment of Women, Young Persons and Children Act 1920**, and the **Children and Young Persons Act 1933**. The former listed occupations in mining, manufacturing, construction and transportation which were to be closed to young people under 14. The 1933 Act stated, with minor exceptions, that no child below the age of 13 was to be employed, and restricted the number of hours that could be worked by young people under school-leaving age. It empowered local authorities to amend some of these rules through the creation of bye-laws which further limited the hours and type of employment undertaken by young people. The result of this has been a variation in the bye-laws and in the extent to which they have been enforced.

From a survey carried out in 1995, it is estimated that more than 40 per cent of children have some form of employment, other than babysitting, running errands and other activities not covered by the law. Of these children, it is thought that almost three-quarters are working illegally, i.e. they are below the age of 13, they are working outside those hours permitted by law and they work in trades proscribed for children. It is estimated that only about a fifth of working children are actually registered for employment and that many are paid at a rate which is seen as exploitative. There is also concern over the number of accidents affecting children at work. Thirty-five per cent of children in one survey reported an accident at work during the preceding year.

A discussion of the problems surrounding young people and part-time work, including details of the 1995 survey, may be found in *The Hidden Army, Children at Work in the 1990s*, published by the Low Pay Unit, and *Children and Work in the UK: reassessing the Issues*, published by the Child Poverty Action Group, 1998.

THE LESSON

1.   The way we were

This section (pages 130 to 131) outlines the situation of many children a century-and-a-half ago. It can be used to introduce the subject or, later, to highlight the value of the legislation and some of the difficulties enforcing it.

2.   Newspaper advertisements

Read through FIND-A-JOB (page 131) with the class. Ask students to study the classified advertisements and decide which of the jobs could be legally offered to someone aged 15. Some help is given in WHAT THE LAW SAYS (page 134). At this stage students would find a copy of the local bye-laws very useful. Separate answer sheets are provided on pages 132 and 133 for both teacher and student use.

3.   Small groups

Read the section PART-TIME WORK TODAY (page 135) with the class and ask students to think about the paid work they or their friends have undertaken. The suggested activities and summary statements prompt students to think about what the law should say on this subject and why.

The discussion cards on page 135 may be useful, particularly for those students who find discussion more difficult. Give each group of students a set of cards and ask them to distinguish between those statements they agree with and those they disagree with. If the group is divided or uncertain, they should discuss the statement fully and try to reach a group decision. Those statements that they agree with should be of some help in devising their summary statement about what the law should be.

4.   Case studies

Read the final section TIP OF THE ICEBERG? (pages 136 and 137) with the class. It points out that in this field the law is frequently flouted. You could discuss these findings and compare them with the students' own experiences. Surveys could be undertaken into the nature and extent of part-time work by school students, although note that this could raise the sensitive issue of particular students being illegally employed.

THE GRIM DEATH TOLL FROM SMOKING

DYING FOR A CIGARETTE?

FROM OUR MEDICAL CORRESPONDENT

ABOUT 25 PER CENT of adults smoke regularly. As a result, they can expect to be ill more and die earlier than non-smokers. About half of all regular smokers will eventually be killed by their habit, with many suffering years of ill-health before they die.

The main killers from smoking are lung cancer, lung disease and heart disease, although doctors say that smoking has around 20 ways of killing you and over 50 ways of making you ill. Every year, smoking kills around 120,000 in UK as a whole. That's 40 times more people than are killed on the roads.

Many doctors have urged the Government to take strong measures to reduce the levels of smoking. Increasingly, laws have been passed to reduce the amount of advertising of cigarette products. As a result, advertising has fallen and warnings on cigarette packets have grown larger and more gruesome. In 2001, the EU passed a new law requiring that in future health warnings must cover between 30 per cent and 40 per cent of the packet. Misleading words such as 'light' and 'mild' will also be banned.

Costs of the habit

In the course of a lifetime, someone who smokes 20 cigarettes a day for 50 years, could expect to spend a total of £75,000. The cost of smoking to the National Health Service is around £1.5 billion.

However, the government makes £10 billion a year from taxing smoking. In the UK 80 per cent of the price of a packet is tax, the highest percentage in Europe. So, the country's finances do well out of this deadly habit. Does this justify doing nothing to stop this habit which can also increase impotence and infertility? Nearly 25 per cent of England's young people seem to think it's worth the risk. And it's their life - or is it?

YOUNG PEOPLE AND SMOKING – FACT FILE

DID YOU KNOW?

☆ In the UK about 500 children start smoking every day.

☆ A study in 1999 found that: 3 per cent of 12-year-olds, 12 per cent of 14-year-olds and 23 per cent of 15-year-olds were regular smokers, which is almost as high as the figure for adult smokers.

☆ During the 1990s the largest increase in numbers of young people smoking was amongst girls rather than boys.

☆ Attitudes of parents to smoking has a strong effect on whether children smoke. Children are three times more likely to smoke if both their parents smoke.

☆ Children who smoke are up to six times more likely to suffer breathing problems than those who do not smoke.

☆ Children who begin to smoke quickly become addicted to the nicotine. Those who try to give up suffer withdrawal symptoms just as adults do. 72 per cent of regular smokers aged 11 to 15 said they thought they would find it difficult to give up altogether.

☆ Shopkeepers who sell cigarettes to children under 16 can be fined up to £2,500. However, in 1999 there were only 136 prosecutions and fines were generally less than £400.

☆ Young people in the UK paid over £100 million in tax on cigarettes bought illegally in 1996.

☆ When the Canadians raised the price of cigarettes dramatically in the 1980s, the level of smoking amongst young people fell sharply.

☆ At present it is not illegal for a young person under 16 to smoke.

Figures from Action on Smoking and Health - www.ash.org.uk

FREEDOM TO THE END!

Often when new laws are introduced for health or safety reasons, people object on the grounds that they should be left to decide for themselves. This happened when the laws requiring seatbelts to be worn in cars and laws allowing water boards to add fluoride to drinking water were introduced. In 1986, people became more aware of the dangers of AIDS, which was spreading rapidly. Yet many objected to the idea of being forced to take a test. 'The law should not interfere', is the cry.

Should we pass laws to stop people smoking? Or are there better ways to deal with the issue?

TALKING POINTS

You are a member of a government commission which has been set up to draft harsh new anti-smoking laws. The effect of your new laws must be to reduce smoking dramatically, especially amongst young people. Read the Young People and Smoking fact file before you begin.

Before you decide on your laws you must consider some of the following points:

a)   Can your new laws be enforced reasonably?
b)   What could happen if a large number of people ignored the new laws, as they did when alcohol was banned in the USA in the 1930s?
c)   How far should your laws interfere with a person's freedom to control his or her own life?

GOOD HEALTH!

THE EFFECTS OF ALCOHOL

When someone swallows alcohol it travels to the stomach and is absorbed through the wall of the stomach into the bloodstream. Blood then carries the alcohol to the brain.

Alcohol is a depressant. It slows down the speed at which the brain works. This means that it affects people's reactions, and their ability to drive or operate a machine.

Each year about 14 million working days are lost through people drinking too much.

Some doctors believe that drinking a small amount of alcohol each week can improve health of people over the age of 50.

But men who regularly drink more than 4 units a day, (without two days alcohol-free) and women who drink more than 3 units a day (again without two alcohol-free days) run the risk of seriously damaging their health. The liver, throat, brain, heart and stomach can all be damaged by drinking too much over a long period of time.

HOW MUCH ALCOHOL?

One unit of alcohol is equivalent to:
◆ half a pint of beer
◆ one glass of wine (125ml)
◆ a pub measure of spirits (25ml)
◆ a measure of port or sherry (25ml)

Extra strong beers or lager contain about 3 times as much alcohol as ordinary beer.

DRINK-DRIVING

The effects of drinking depend on the amount of alcohol in a person's bloodstream. This is called the blood alcohol concentration.

The legal limit for driving is 80 milligrammes of alcohol in 100 millilitres of blood. There's no way of being certain how much a person can drink before reaching this limit. This depends on a person's sex, their weight and how fast they have been drinking.

In the United Kingdom, one in five car drivers killed in traffic accidents is over the legal limit. Road accidents after drinking are the biggest cause of death in young men. Drunk drivers are likely to kill not only themselves but others. Many crimes are committed by people who have been drinking.

THANK GOODNESH YOU CAME OSHIFER. CAN YOU GET THISH COW OFF MY CAR?

This type of cartoon makes drink-driving seem like a joke, but in real life it is not so funny.

WHAT'S THE DIFFERENCE?

Compare these two cases. Do you agree with the sentences?

Alan MacDonald, a marketing director, asked the court not to jail him after giving a positive breath test at the wheel of his Ferrari, while on bail for another drink drive charge. Instead he was fined £2,000 and given a six-month sentence, suspended for two years. He would serve the prison sentence if he offended within that period. MacDonald was also given a six-year driving ban. He had three previous convictions for drink driving.

A drink driver who killed a young couple when he hit their car at 70 m.p.h. was jailed for five years and banned from driving for 10 years. John Adams, aged 36, had drunk 10 pints of lager, Preston Crown Court was told. Adams was found guilty of causing death by reckless driving.

WHAT THE LAW SAYS

Under 5 It is an offence to give an alcoholic drink to a child under 5.

Under 14 Children under 14 are not allowed on their own in the bar of a pub, except one which has a 'children's certificate'. This is issued by local magistrates who must be satisfied that the bar is suitable for young children. This usually only lasts until 9.00 pm but this can be varied by the magistrates.

Over 14 Someone over 14 may go into a bar, with the landlord's permission, but may not buy or drink alcohol.

Over 16 Someone over 16 may buy punch, beer, cider, with a meal.

Under 18 It is against the law for anyone under 18 to buy or drink alcohol in a bar - or for an older person to buy a drink for them.

The offence of **drunkenness**
It is an offence to be drunk on any highway, in any public place or licensed premises or at a sports event.

The offence of **drunkenness with aggravation**
This is a more serious offence and includes being drunk and disorderly, being drunk in possession of a firearm or while being in charge of a child under seven.

The Criminal Justice and Police Act 2001
This act was intended to tackle the growing problem of street crime, public disorder and unruly behaviour (sometimes called 'yob culture'). This allows the police to give on-the-spot fines for a range of offences relating to drinking in public.

The Act also gives local authorities the power to make certain public places 'alcohol free zones'. It will be an offence to consume alcohol in such a zone.

The Act says that those who sell alcohol must take 'all reasonable steps' to make sure that their customers are 18. It also gives the police the power to ask under 18s to test whether shopkeepers are willing to sell alcohol to young people under the legal age.

Should the Law be Changed?

- Compared with most other goods, alcoholic drinks are cheaper than they were 25 years ago.

- In England and Wales, 33,000 people a year are dying from causes linked to the drinking of alcohol, including ill health, road crashes, and drunken violence.

- Across Europe, one in eight deaths amongst young men is linked to alcohol.

- Tighter drink-driving laws have reduced the number of deaths on the road in recent years (but the legal limit in Britain is still one third higher than in many European countries).

- One quarter of all people arrested are drunk. Nearly half of all violent crime and three quarters of stabbings are committed after drinking too much. Alcohol is associated with 50 per cent of domestic violence incidents.

- Drinking amongst women is on the increase, along with 'binge-drinking' amongst young people. Britain's 15-year-olds are amongst the highest drinkers in Europe.

- There are few laws banning advertising of drinks in Britain. The drinks industry operates its own code of conduct. For example, it has banned adverts from linking drinks with being macho or feminine. However, it uses many devices like sports sponsorship to link drinking with positive, healthy images.

- The World Health Organisation says that countries which have banned advertising of beer, wines and spirits, consume over 10 per cent less of these drinks.

- The government in England was reported in 2001 to be seriously concerned about under-age drinking and to be planning new ways of tackling the problem.

- Law and order problems rise dramatically on Friday and Saturday nights especially when the pubs close. It has been suggested that allowing alcohol to be available at any time would improve this situation, but others believe that the amount of drinking would increase.

- About two-thirds of the adults in Britain regularly drink alcohol without, it seems, suffering any harm.

MAKING CHOICES

Should anything be done to make people drink less alcohol?

Here are some suggestions.

Tick those that you think are a good idea.

Add any ideas of your own. Which ideas do you think would work best?

1 Make all alcoholic drinks more expensive. This could be done by increasing the tax on drinks.

2 Ban all advertising on alcoholic drinks.

3 Allow the police to stop motorists at any time to check they are not driving under the influence of drink. (At the moment the police must reasonably suspect someone to have been drinking before they can be stopped.)

4 Give harsh punishments to anyone who sells alcohol to a young person who is under age.

5 Run a big educational campaign to encourage everyone to drink less alcohol.

6 Make alcohol illegal, like some other drugs.

7 Introduce compulsory carrying of identity cards.

8 Leave things as they are and do nothing.

ARGUING A CASE

The subject of alcohol and the way it is used is a complicated one. Some people are very strongly against it whilst others think it is just a part of everyday life.

In this exercise you will be asked to write a letter to a local paper in favour of a particular point of view. It will probably not be your own opinion but you should still try to present as convincing a case as possible. Choose facts and figures to support the case you are arguing. If you can, you should also try to answer some of the points against you.

Try to use as much evidence as possible to support your case. Think about what tactics you might use in your letter, such as appealing to the emotions by using accident statistics. Use any additional arguments or experiences of your own, if they are relevant.

ROLE CARD 1

You are someone who does not drink alcohol at all. Argue that the recent rise in alcohol consumption is dangerous and the government should do something about it.

ROLE CARD 2

You are a teacher and are concerned that young people are drinking too much. Make some suggestions about what might be done.

ROLE CARD 3

You know someone who has been seriously injured in a road accident in which one of the drivers had drunk too much. Argue that the laws about drinking and driving should be tightened up and that there should be less pressure to drink.

ROLE CARD 4

You like a drink to help you relax at home and at parties. You are not in favour of drinking too much but you believe that people should be free to make up their own minds. Argue the case against tightening up the laws controlling the drinking of alcohol.

WORK AND PLAY

THE WAY WE WERE

The year is 1840. A government inspector arrives in Halifax, in Yorkshire, to find out what it is like for children working in the coal mines.

He goes underground and is horrified by what he finds:
"I have had to creep upon my hands and knees the whole distance, the height being barely twenty inches, and then have gone still lower upon my breast and crawled like a turtle to get up to the headings (the coal face)."

"Children, as well as men and women, crawl through these tunnels all day long. They haul coal from where the miners work back to the shafts. Girls pull the wagons by means of a belt worn around the waist with a chain passing

between the legs. They move forward by crawling on their hands and knees." Most people knew nothing of the conditions in which children worked in the mines.

Some children work hauling coal for their fathers. Many are treated no better than if they worked for others. The inspector discovers Elizabeth Eggley (aged 15) loading for her father. She picks up a piece of coal weighing 45 kg and carries it a metre to the truck. Her father does nothing to help. It is very hot below ground. Children and adults have to strip off to try and keep cool. Mary Barrett (aged 14) reports:

"I always work without stockings or shoes, or trousers. I wear nothing but my shift; I have to go up the headings with the men, they are all naked there."

The inspector asks how the children are treated. Margaret Gormley (aged 12) replies:

"They flog us down in the pit, which hurts me very much; Thomas Copeland flogs me more than once in a day, which makes me cry."

Injury and death were common in the mines.

◆ Why do you think young people are, or have been, made to work?
◆ Why do you think young people want to work?
◆ Do young people these days need to work?

FIND-A-JOB

Look at the advertisements for part-time jobs and decide which of them could be legally offered to someone of 15. The information on page 134 will help you. So too, will a copy of your local bye-laws which control the employment of young people in your area.

BABYSITTER WANTED
to look after two children, age 6 and 7, every Sunday night. Good pay for suitable person. Box No. 32.

FRUIT AND VEGETABLE PICKERS
wanted, during the school summer holidays. Piece rates.
Contact Mr Luck, Grange Farm.
Tel: 868 414.

HAIRDRESSER
offers Saturday work 8.30am-4.30pm for smart young person.
Phone Kim at Shades, Cannon Square.
Tel 958 232

WINDOW CLEANER requires assistant, Saturday mornings only. Suit fit young person.
Tel: 840 478.

PAPER ROUNDS available.
Start 7am, mornings only. Seven days a week. Call: Benn's paper shop, Bridgegate.

GARAGE CASHIER AND ATTENDANT required. Local busy garage. Part-time work, hours to suit. Hodgson's, London Road. Tel: 506367.

MARKET TRADER needs young person to work on vegetable stall. Saturdays 8am-4pm. Good pay.
Tel: 703 747.

SKYLIGHTS RESTAURANT
needs smart young person to serve customers. Friday and Saturday evenings. Tel: 700 220.

BABYSITTER

Babysitting for friends and neighbours, even for money, is not usually regarded as employment. However it might be, if a young person was childminding for two hours each day after school. Present laws do not prevent young people under 16 from doing this kind of work, but if something went wrong it is likely that a court would judge that a babysitter or childminder under 16 was not fit for such a job. In this case, the parents would be at fault for not arranging for their children to be properly cared for.

FRUIT AND VEGETABLE PICKERS

This work may be offered to a 15-year-old, as long as it does not involve heavy strain or the operation of dangerous machinery. Local bye-laws will also state the maximum number of hours that the young person may work during the week.

HAIRDRESSER

The bye-laws of most areas do not allow a young person to work in a hairdresser's until they have reached school-leaving age. However, the **Education (Work Experience) Act 1973** allows students on work experience to do certain jobs for which they would otherwise have to be 16. Working in a hairdresser's would come into this category.

MARKET TRADER

Generally young people under 17 are not allowed to work as street traders or in an open-air market, unless they are 14 years or over and employed by their parents and it is permitted by the local bye-laws. Other than this, all kinds of street trading are forbidden to young people and this includes selling fruit or vegetables by the roadside.

Paper Round

The young person would be allowed to have a paper round as long as it did not interfere with the start of the school day. The local bye-laws will state how long the round may last. This is often for a period of one hour or until 8.30 am. No young person is permitted to work before 7.00 am.

Garage Attendant

Most bye-laws forbid this. Some ban the delivery and serving of fuel, while others just prohibit the delivery of fuel by people below school-leaving age. Other regulations governing garage forecourts also apply here, many forbid young people below 15 from close contact with petrol.

Skylights Restaurant

Most bye-laws allow 15-year-olds to serve food, but work in the kitchens of any hotel, restaurant or take-away is normally forbidden. However, this job should not be offered to a 15-year-old as it involves working after 7.00pm and almost certainly for more than two hours on a school day.

Window Cleaner

Most local bye-laws state that young people below school-leaving age may not clean outside windows more than 3 or 4 metres above the ground. So unless the work was inside, or only on the ground floors, the young person could not take this job.

WHAT THE LAW SAYS

YOUNG PEOPLE AT WORK

Most of the law which applies to young people working part-time while at school is set down in the **Children and Young Persons Act 1933**. As a general rule, this states that no children under the age of 13 may be employed. It also lists the times that young people between 13 and school-leaving age may work. No young person may work:

● during school hours on any school day
● before 7.00 am and after 7.00 pm
● for more than two hours on any school day
● for more than two hours on a Sunday.

Local laws

The Act also allows local councils to pass bye-laws which can further restrict the work young people can do. These bye-laws are often similar, but not always. In Doncaster, South Yorkshire, for example, children may do light farm work in the company of their parents from the age of 10. Five miles away, in Nottinghamshire, the age is 12.

Enforcing the law

It is mainly the duty of the local education authority to make sure that the law is being obeyed. Many local authorities require employers to write to them giving the name, address, job and hours of the young person who is working for them. The young person's parents must give permission for their child to work and a medical certificate of fitness must be sent to the education office within two weeks of starting work. If everything is correct, the council gives the young person an Employment Card, which he or she should be ready to show to an official at any time during work. Employers and young people who break this law may be fined.

Ignoring the law

Studies have shown that the law is ignored by many employers. Many young people have been found to be illegally employed. This can present serious problems in case of accident.

Part-Time Work Today – an Investigation

Carry out your own investigation into young people's part-time work.

Your questions could ask about:
- ◆ the hours young people work
- ◆ their wages, and whether they vary for different types of work
- ◆ people's knowledge of the law
- ◆ whether employers follow the correct procedures when employing young people.

Use your findings to help you decide what you think the law should say about young people at work.

Discussion Cards

DISCUSSION CARD 1
Children should be allowed to work for their parents at any age.

DISCUSSION CARD 2
Work can interfere with young people's schooling by making them tired or late for school.

DISCUSSION CARD 3
The law should not stop young people from working in any job they can find.

DISCUSSION CARD 4
Work helps young people to be more independent and teaches them how to look after themselves.

DISCUSSION CARD 5
Wages given to young people are often too low. There should be a minimum wage for 14-18-year-olds.

DISCUSSION CARD 6
There are some jobs which should be forbidden to young people by law.

TIP OF THE ICEBERG?

Although the law controlling the employment of young people is often broken, very few employers are taken to court. Part of the problem is the small number of inspectors. Another is the fact that many young people want to earn money and are 'willing victims'.

A survey carried out in 1995 showed that about 40 per cent of children work part-time, but about three-quarters of these are employed illegally because they were either: too young, working illegal hours or not following proper safety procedures.

Look at the cases below. Mark on the page or write down those ways in which the law has been broken. Decide whether you think any legal action should be taken against those involved. If so, who would you prosecute? – the employer, the parents, or the young person?

CAR CRAZY

Tom Harrop's job is to do cars up and sell them as fast as he can. Much of his help with this comes from Steve, who's 14. Each Saturday and Sunday and most days in the holiday you will find Steve working on one of Tom's cars.

"Tom lets me do quite a bit now," says Steve. "I jack up the cars, change the wheels and do all the routine maintenance. Last weekend he let me help him spray a van. That was good, but the smell of the paint made me feel a bit sick."

What does he like best? "It's good having some money of your own," replies Steve, "but the best part is learning about, and driving the cars."

OVERTIME AT THE SUPERMARKET

Graham will be 15 this month. He lives in a mining village in South Yorkshire. His dad used to work in the local pit until he was injured in an accident three years ago. His mum works full-time looking after Graham's three younger sisters.

By 4.30pm Graham has come home from school, changed, had some tea and has started work at the local supermarket. At 9.00pm he walks back home, after an evening of filling shelves, unloading vans and shifting boxes.

Graham enjoys his work and the money. With a full day's work on Saturday, he brings home more than £70 a week.

What about his homework? "It's not set every day," says Graham, "but I usually get some done first thing in the morning or just before I go to bed at night, if I can stay awake."

15-YEAR-OLD MANAGER

Seven children and 20 adults are employed in a factory in the West Midlands making 4,000 shoes a week. Much of the time the business is run by the owner's 15-year-old daughter who spends up to seven hours a day at the factory. She misses a great deal of school. Her two sisters, aged 11 and 14, each work on pressing and folding machines at the factory.

Their father praises their work: "The children are very hard workers, much better than grown-ups. We work from 7.00am every day until the job is finished." He added that his factory is able to sell shoes for about £10 a pair less than other firms.

UNIT 9

IT'S THE LAW!

This unit helps students to

◆ explore a number of issues surrounding the law, the values on which it is based and the way in which it is enforced;

◆ examine the law of theft and consider several legal and moral dilemmas to do with respect for property and the law;

◆ examine various aspects of juvenile crime and how the police and courts deal with young people;

◆ consider issues around policing and the role of the public in enforcing the law.

TOPIC ONE

THE ISLAND

AIMS

◆ To encourage pupils to consider ways of resolving conflict;

◆ To look at the relationship between laws and cultural values and human rights.

BACKGROUND

In this topic, students undertake a simulation in which an island is reached by settlers whose rules and laws are very different from those of the indigenous inhabitants. Taking on the roles of community members they identify points of difference and attempt to resolve the conflicts through negotiation. Students are then faced with the problem of framing new laws, which respect the cultural values of both communities.

The cultural background of the Islanders and Settlers closely corresponds to that of the Aborigines and English settlers on Tasmania in the early nineteenth century. The outcome of this conflict is the basis of the work in the next topic, Van Diemen's Land.

THE LESSON

1.   An island

Study the map on page 155 and ask pupils to imagine an island which, for many years, has been cut off from the rest of the world. Its inhabitants have carried on their way of life for centuries unaffected by events in neighbouring countries. Then, searching for new land and better opportunities, a group of settlers reaches the island. They send word home, encouraging others to join them, and in a short time a community of about 1,000 people has been established.

2.   Small groups

Divide the class into two equal groups. Inform one group that it is to take on the role of the **Islanders**, the established community on the island. Tell the other that it will be the **Settlers**, the newcomers to the island. Further divide each half into groups of two or three pupils, but make sure that the same number of small groups exists in each half.

Give students details of their community (page 156 or 157 and 158). Do not go through these details with the whole class - initially the Islanders and the Settlers should remain ignorant of each other's way of life.

3.   Decision cards

Now provide each small group of Islanders and Settlers with its own set of **DECISION CARDS**, cut up from page 159. The cards are numbered 1 to 6. Each numbered card refers to the same event, seen from either the Settlers' or the Islanders' point of view. Ask pupils to read each card and sort them into two piles. On one pile they should place those cards which describe events which they think should be allowed to take place in their community. On the other, they should place the cards describing events which they believe should not be allowed to take place, according to their own values or beliefs.

4.   Role play

Each small group of Islanders and Settlers should now meet with its opposite number to try to resolve their differences. To this meeting they should bring the cards containing details of the incidents to which they object, according to the customs and laws of their community. Encourage pupils to search for solutions which have the support of both sides. Draw the class together and ask individual groups what decisions they managed to reach.

On page 160 there is some guidance as to how the Islanders and the Settlers might each have regarded these incidents.

5.   Written work

Ask pupils to explain the new rules they have developed for the Islanders and the Settlers. These could be presented as a list or poster using only signs and symbols (given the absence of a shared written language).

6.   Class discussion

Finish the lesson by asking the class what will happen if agreement cannot be reached between both communities. Whose way of life is likely to become dominant?

VAN DIEMEN'S LAND

Pupils are shown how the situation they have been discussing in the first topic parallels the conflict between the Aborigines and Settlers in nineteenth century Van Diemen's Land (Tasmania). They learn about the annihilation of the Aborigines and consider some of the legal and moral issues it raises.

AIMS

◆   **To examine the causes and the consequences of the failure of two communities to resolve their differences peaceably;**

◆   **To consider the breaches of human rights suffered by the Aboriginal people.**

BACKGROUND

Students are shown the real outcome of the simulation they undertook in the previous topic. They are asked to consider reasons why the situation arose and some ways in which acts of racial discrimination might be prevented.

The first British settlement on Van Diemen's Land was established in 1803 at Sullivan's Cove. This is now the site of the island's capital, Hobart. Estimates of the size of the Aboriginal population at this time vary, but most authorities estimate it to be around 4,000 people.

In establishing a settlement, the settlers cleared and fenced off land for their crops and animals and treated this land as their own property. This notion of property was alien to Aborigines who owned no land (in the European sense) and had no possessions other than a weapon and a drinking vessel. They commonly shared food and other necessities between all members of the community in which they lived.

The land was of great cultural importance to the Aborigines as it represented the resting place of their ancestors. They believed the land was merely entrusted to them for safe keeping before being handed on, intact, to the next generation. The differences between the two cultures were so fundamental that some form of conflict was unavoidable.

Following the arrival of the settlers in Tasmania, there was a sharp decline in the Aboriginal population. It was increasingly difficult for Aborigines to maintain their livelihood. Many were shot or poisoned, and some were hunted for sport. Many also died from European diseases. In 1830 about 2,000 remained, and by 1835 this figure had fallen to 150.

By the 1850s the authorities in Britain had recognised the scale and the injustice of the human destruction, but attempts to redress the situation were too little and too late. Some legislation was enacted but there was clearly a lack of public will to make it work and the remaining Aborigines gradually died of disease and drink, their reason for existence having been removed with their land.

It was at about this time that the name of the island was changed to Tasmania to remove the association of Van Diemen's Land with lawlessness and disorder.

Persecution of the Aborigines in mainland Australia continued well into the twentieth century. In some remote areas, where the Aborigines had been able to maintain their traditional way of life, the mass murder of Aboriginal folk was not unknown. Two major incidents, in 1926 and 1928, where parties of police slaughtered eleven and thirty-one Aborigines respectively, provoked considerable public outrage, although no white person was ever brought to trial.

Whilst these atrocities were the last of this kind, other less violent forms of discrimination and oppression continued. For example, during the 1920s and 1930s, the Aborigines' Protection Board devised a policy whereby Aboriginal children were taken from their parents and brought up separately in institutions. It was hoped that this way 'full blood' Aborigines would die out within one or two generations on their reserves. Economic and political power was also withheld from Aborigines. For example, until the mid 1970s in Queensland, Aborigines' wages were put into a trust fund and administered by the police.

THE LESSON

1.   A real-life conflict

Explain to students that the simulation they have just undertaken closely mirrors a real-life conflict between the Tasmanian Aborigines and settlers from England during the nineteenth century. Read through the information on pages 161 and 162 with students and ask them to indicate how they coped with the problems in their earlier role play.

Explain that the seventeenth, eighteenth and nineteenth centuries were periods of colonial expansion by many European nations. Lands were acquired for individual and national gain, usually with no understanding of the culture of the indigenous peoples and little regard for their human rights. There were also undoubtedly prejudices amongst the settlers about the Aborigines, compounded by language barriers and an almost complete failure to comprehend their nomadic and non-materialistic way of life.

2.   Class discussion

Read the remainder of the story, on page 163, with the class and raise the question of the rights of those who wish to settle in a new country and of those who receive newcomers onto their land. What rights do the students believe should belong to both sides? What happened to the Aborigines gives a graphic example of how institutional racism works and provides another perspective on those who emigrate to escape death or persecution and those who seek an better life. Help students relate those issues to current events in the UK.

On pages 164 and 165, there is a brief note on the Aboriginal people today, together with extracts from the **United Nations Declaration of Human Rights**. These may provide a positive framework for the discussion of a variety of issues connected with race and conflict between ethnic groups.

RESOURCES

Dispossession, Black Australians and White Invaders, Henry Reynolds, Allen and Unwin. This interesting collection of contemporary quotations provides an insight into how white Australians viewed the Aborigines. Not suitable for pupil use.

The Fatal Shore, Robert Hughes, Harvil. An account of the 160,000 women, men and children who left Britain for Australia during the last century. Several chapters specifically deal with the impact of the settlers on the Tasmanian Aboriginal people.

Aboriginal Australians, Kieth Suter and Kaye Stearman, Minority Rights Group. Examines the treatment of Aboriginal Australians in the areas of health, education, laws and access to land. 3rd edition 1988 (reprint with update 1994), 0946690618, 22pp (plus 4pp insert).
Available through bookshops or direct from Minority Rights Group, 379 Brixton Road, London SW9 7DE, 020 7978 9498, www.minorityrights.org.

Information on the *Universal Declaration of Human Rights* is available from the United Nations Information Centre, 20 Buckingham Gate, London SWIE 6LB, 020 7630 1981, www.unitednations.org.uk.

Amnesty International is a worldwide movement working for human rights. Many schools have Amnesty groups which campaign and raise awareness of human rights. Information is available from Amnesty International, British Section, 99-119 Rosebery Avenue, London EC1R 4RE, 020 7278 6000, www.amnesty.org.uk.

IS IT THEFT?

AIMS

◆ To introduce pupils to the law of theft;

◆ To consider the relationship between the legal and moral responsibilities involved in respecting other people's property.

BACKGROUND

This topic is divided into two sections. Students are introduced to the law of theft and then they are provided with four familiar situations where money or goods are acquired by accident or otherwise. They are asked to decide whether, by keeping the items, the individual has committed an act of theft.

A LITTLE EXTRA is based upon a 1988 court case in which a man was accused of theft, having been wrongly credited with an extra £20,000 by his building society. This case has been chosen to introduce pupils to the basic legal definition of theft.

The legal definition of theft is contained in the **Theft Act 1968**. Section 1 (1) states: 'A person is guilty of theft if he dishonestly appropriates property belonging to another with the intention of permanently depriving the other of it'. In the pupils' materials, this definition is broken down into three essential parts - dishonesty, taking or keeping property belonging to someone else, and the intent permanently to deprive the owner of that property. If one of these elements is absent, a court should not convict a person of theft.

In a criminal case, the case against the accused should be proved beyond reasonable doubt. This is a higher level of proof than is required in a civil case where the test is the balance of probabilities. There is in law an assumption that it is better to allow a guilty person to go free than to unjustly punish someone who is innocent. In a criminal case, the burden of proof lies with the prosecution, not the defence. In other words, the defence only has to cast doubt on the prosecution's case. It does not have to prove innocence.

THE LESSON

1.   **A case study**

Read through the case **A LITTLE EXTRA** (page 166) with your class and check that the details are clearly understood. Before asking pupils to reach a verdict it is important to explain the three criteria which form the basis of the legal definition of theft (see page 167). To find John guilty, pupils must be certain that all the essential elements are present. They must be certain that he took or kept something belonging to someone else, and that he did not intend to return it, and that he behaved dishonestly.

2.   **Class discussion**

When pupils have reached a verdict, compare answers and check that they have applied the criteria for theft in a systematic way. Pupils are likely to be more successful with later sections if these details have been clearly understood.

Tell students that, after a three-day trial, the jury found the accused not guilty of theft. Juries are not called upon to give a reason for their verdict, but we can presume that John's attempts to draw the error to the attention of the building society convinced the jury that he had not behaved with dishonest intent. The importance to the verdict of the honesty of the accused can be underlined by asking pupils if their decision would have been different had John not tried to tell the building society staff about their mistake.

Although the defendant was found not guilty of theft, there still remained the question of whether he should return to the building society the money that he had already spent. It was not within the power of the Crown Court to deal with this and the building society needed to bring a fresh case through a civil court to reclaim the money.

3.   **Extension activity**

As an extension to this work, ask pupils each to record, on a slip of paper, whether they would demand the return of the money. Before voting, elicit from the class the arguments both for and against the return of the funds.

4.   **Small groups**

Provide each group of students with page 169, entitled **OWNING UP**, cut into slips. Each slip outlines an incident involving a member of a family. Students should place the slips in a pile face down on the desk and go through each one in turn, deciding whether the law has been broken. Students will probably need to be reminded of the three elements essential to the legal definition of theft - particularly if any time has elapsed since their work on the previous section, **A LITTLE EXTRA**. Groups can record their verdict on page 168 along with the reasons for their decision. When students have had time to complete their answers give them each a copy of page 170, which outlines the legal details behind each case. Be prepared to devote some time to this, as the distinctions made in law, particularly over intent, can be rather subtle.

5.   **Class discussion**

After each legal explanation, students are asked what they feel they might have done in a similar position. The dilemmas created by these situations can be exposed as you take the class through each case, or left until the legal considerations have been completed. For example, in the first case, ask pupils if their answers would have been different had the dinner lady been a neighbour or relation of Michael's, or in the third case if Carl had worked for a charity. The gap between the 'finder' and the 'loser' can be similarly closed in the other examples - where perhaps the money lost by Rosie is found by a friend, and the spanners found in Lucy's car belong to a colleague at work who has repaired her car as a favour.

6.   **Extension activity**

The reactions of finders and losers can be examined further as a piece of extended writing or role play which might begin at the point where the dinner lady realises she has made a mistake, or where the workshop manager of the garage telephones Lucy to ask if she has found any tools in her car which don't belong to her.

TOPIC FOUR

A NICE LITTLE EARNER

AIM

     To help pupils decide upon a just outcome in a case of theft.

BACKGROUND

Ella and Tom, both 13, start a part-time job delivering newspapers, but soon begin taking goods from the shop and selling them to their friends. A teacher at their school discovers what they are doing and informs the head teacher. Students explore the reactions of those involved and try to determine a just outcome to the case.

Although in the story neither Mr Wakefield nor the head teacher chooses to inform the police, police officers do from time to time visit schools in the investigation of offences. The procedure for this is governed by the **Codes of Practice** for the **Police and Criminal Evidence Act 1984**. In these codes, which are non-statutory and can be found in local police stations and libraries, it states, 'juveniles may only be interviewed at their place of education in exceptional circumstances and then only where the principal or his nominee agrees and is present'. In this case a police officer would interview Tom or Ella only in the presence of their parents or nominees. It is also stated in the codes that 'a juvenile should not be arrested at his place of education unless this is unavoidable. In this case the principal or his nominee must be informed'.

Police officers, solicitors, magistrates and local business people can provide further information about the consequences of theft.

THE LESSON

1.   **A story**

Ask students to read the story **A NICE LITTLE EARNER** (pages 171 and 172), which is based on fact. Check that they understand it, and ask them to decide what the head teacher should do, having learnt of Tom's and Ella's alleged offence.

2.   **Class discussion**

Ask students to indicate what they would do first, and what they would not do at all. There are opportunities here to discuss questions of fairness - the head teacher must not immediately assume that Ella and Tom are guilty. The class could also consider the appropriateness of calling in the police to investigate such incidents in a school.

Indicate to the class what the law says and point out that it is not only Tom and Ella who have committed an offence, but possibly also those who have bought stolen goods from them. The offence of receiving stolen goods applies to those who knowingly obtain the proceeds of theft. A bona fide purchaser is exempt from this, but may find difficulty in establishing the facts in court.

3.   **Small groups**

Use **REACTIONS**, page 173, to ask students to explore what each of the main characters in this story might be thinking. If they are working in groups, encourage students to share their ideas, discuss feelings and give reasons before they decide what to write down.

4.   **Role play**

If time allows, these notes can form the basis of a short piece of drama which takes place when Tom and Ella are confronted by their parents, or meet Mr Wakefield to explain what they have done. Ask students to consider what they think should happen to the culprits.

5.   **Class discussion**

Now give students page 174, **A NOT SO NICE LITTLE EARNER**, where it is explained how the incident was actually concluded. Some pupils will be surprised that Mr Wakefield appeared to forgive Ella and Tom and offered them the chance to continue working for him. Ask students to think about why he might have reacted in this way. Do they think it would have been better to have called the police? Would this have been a fairer outcome, and would it have been more beneficial to Ella and Tom? In this way the lesson can be extended to consider the purposes of punishment and how such offenders should be treated.

Finally, ask the class in pairs, groups, and then as a whole class, to list all the reasons why it is wrong to steal. Reasons will probably include eg, 'Because you will get caught' and reasons which focus on the victim. Ask students to sort the reasons into those which are concerned for self and those which recognize the effect of crime on others. Ask them which reasons are better and why they think this. The issue also provides an opportunity to think about forgiveness, including how hard it is and the possible effect on those forgiven.

TOPIC FIVE

YOUNG PEOPLE AND CRIME

AIMS

◆ **To consider the nature of juvenile crime and of the effects of crime on young people as victims;**

◆ **To introduce court procedures as they affect young people.**

BACKGROUND

Police policy with regard to cautioning juveniles differs from force to force. You may wish to involve a local police officer or solicitor in the teaching of this topic.

THE LESSON

1.   **Class discussion**

Look at the graphs of crime figures on page 175 with the class. Ask students to think of possible reasons to explain the high rate of recorded juvenile crime. Then look at the list of reasons given on page 176 and discuss the points raised on the page. The discussion is couched in general terms but if your relationship with your class is good, it may be more fruitful to open up the areas of juveniles' motives and the pressures they are under to commit crimes. It is also important to consider young people as victims of crime and to discuss it as a shared problem which seriously affects people's lives.

2.   **A case study**

Pages 177 to 179 deal with what happens when a young person is arrested and look at the main provisions of the **Police and Criminal Evidence Act 1984** with special reference to young people. The main purpose of this material is to discuss the protection offered by the law and the powers of the police, in relation to those suspected of committing a crime.

The picture story concerns the arrest and questioning of Louise Jones at the police station and examines the procedures which follow.
Read the story with the class and discuss the questions raised.

3.   **Class discussion**

Read page 180 **WHICH SENTENCE?** with the class and ask students to think how a young person like Louise should be treated in the judicial process. The tariff given does not represent the whole range of sentences which may be given to a young person but only those from which a magistrate is likely to select for such an offence. (Pages 181 and 182 provide students with further information on police powers.)

OUT OF THE BLUE

AIM

◆ To introduce the broad scope of police work and consider the nature of the contribution the police make to the community.

BACKGROUND

Pupils consider evidence from the police strikes of 1918 and 1919 to examine the role of the police and the wide variety of tasks they undertake.

During the years of the First World War, the pay of police officers had not kept up with the rise in the cost of living. By 1918, many officers were paid so little that they and their families were undernourished. In such a state, some were tempted to take bribes and offers of food in return for favours. Pay was not the only complaint. Working hours were long and badly arranged, and during the first six months of the War, most officers lost 17 days' leave. This had been arbitrarily cancelled, causing great anger. With an increasingly long list of grievances, many officers felt very discontented. For some years there had been a small, but illegal police union, and when one of its members, Thomas Thiel, was sacked it proved to be the spark which drew large numbers of officers into industrial action. Union membership soared, and the union leaders wrote to the Prime Minister, Lloyd George, demanding:

● more money;
● that the sacked officer should be taken back;
● that the police union should be allowed to operate openly.

It was August, and despite the nation being at war, many senior government ministers and staff were on holiday, and those who were left seemed to think that the police were bluffing. They were not, and on 30 August 1918, 6,000 Metropolitan police officers went on strike. A large crowd of strikers marched to Downing Street and a small delegation was admitted to speak to the Prime Minister. In the Cabinet Room, the government gave the impression of complete surrender to the strikers. Thomas Thiel was reinstated, pay and pensions were increased and the government agreed to the establishment of an organisation to represent the officers, when the war was over.

A year later, police officers were again complaining of low pay. The government set up a committee to report on pay and conditions, but continued to resist their demand for the establishment of a trade union. Some officers joined together to strike against this measure, but support was much less than it had been in the previous year. In August 1919, 2,634 men from seven forces came out on strike. The area most affected was Liverpool.

The strike resulted in immediate trouble on Merseyside. There was severe rioting. Tanks and troops in battle dress were sent in to quell the mob. There were reports of bayonet charges and bloodshed and one man was fatally wounded. However, support for the strike across the country was not forthcoming and other unions failed to support the strikers. After 24 hours, the strike collapsed. All the striking officers lost their jobs. Not one was reinstated.

THE LESSON

1. A newspaper story

Read pages 183 and 184 with the class, and introduce the information on the police strikes. Ask students to indicate who they feel was to blame for the strike and whether the police should have been allowed to form a trade union.

In the remaining questions on page 184, students are asked to imagine the likely consequences of a police strike today. It is suggested that they consider this in terms of themselves and their family and the wider community in which they live. It is likely that their immediate thoughts will revolve around problems of crime and public order, but encourage pupils to think about the many other areas of community life in which the police become involved (such as seeking missing persons, traffic control, informing families about victims of accidents, advising on security and so on). Use the expertise of a police officer, if available, to provide evidence of the wide variety of activities an officer might engage in during the course of a normal working day.

2. Class discussion

Draw together pupils' ideas and summarise the main effects envisaged by the class. It may be interesting to raise in discussion the question of our basic morality and ask pupils what they think prevents most people, for most of the time, from acting in a 'lawless' way. Is it the police, the law, fear of being caught or more positive feelings of respect for others or the rule of law?

NEW RECRUITS

AIM

◆ **To consider the personal qualities needed by police officers.**

BACKGROUND

Students draw up a list of qualities they would be like to see in new recruits to the police service.

It may be helpful to arrange for the assistance of a local police officer during this lesson.

THE LESSON

Class discussion

Give out page 185 and draw students' attention to the details in the top half of the page, showing the range of work undertaken by the police and the numbers of officers in the force.

Now ask students to consider the qualities they feel are necessary to be a good police officer. Ask them also to decide what percentage of the police force should be represented by women and members of ethnic minority groups.

If possible, arrange for a local police officer to answer the same questions, for comparison with those of the rest of the class. Also, if time allows, try to provide pupils with an opportunity to raise questions of their own with the officer (having planned and discussed their questions in advance).

ACTION STATIONS

AIMS

◆ To examine some of the issues raised when people decide to take the law into their own hands;

◆ To consider the role of individuals and the public in enforcing the law.

BACKGROUND

Students propose measures for dealing with a serious outbreak of theft in a community, and consider the role of neighbourhood patrols in combatting crime.

A citizen has the power to arrest a person whom she or he believes has committed an arrestable offence. This is usually an offence which carries the maximum penalty of five or more years' imprisonment.

Unlike a police officer, a citizen may not arrest someone merely on suspicion of committing a crime nor someone who is about to commit a crime, but has not yet committed it.

A residents' patrol group may therefore be able to arrest someone who has broken into a house and is leaving with stolen goods, but may not arrest a person carrying a bag and tools on the suspicion that a crime is about to be committed. In such circumstances the man or woman with the bag could sue the citizen for wrongful arrest.

THE LESSON

1.   **Small groups**

Give out **LOCAL RESIDENTS ARE FURIOUS** page 186 and outline the situation faced by local residents. Ask students, at first individually and then in small groups, to make a list of all the things that can be done to make the community safer. Encourage students to think about the problem as widely as possible. Draw up a plan of action by taking one suggestion from each small group.

2.   **Two newspaper stories**

Give out pages 187 and 188, **TAKING THE LAW INTO THEIR OWN HANDS**, and go through both newspaper stories with the class. These give contrasting accounts of how an apparent rise in crime was handled by two actual community groups. Compare these with the students' own action plans and ask how they would react to the community groups' action plans if they were local residents in Milton Yardley or Grimethorpe. Encourage students to explain their concerns and to suggest what other measures could have been taken to protect local citizens.

THE ISLAND

Look at the map below. It will give you some idea of what the island is like.

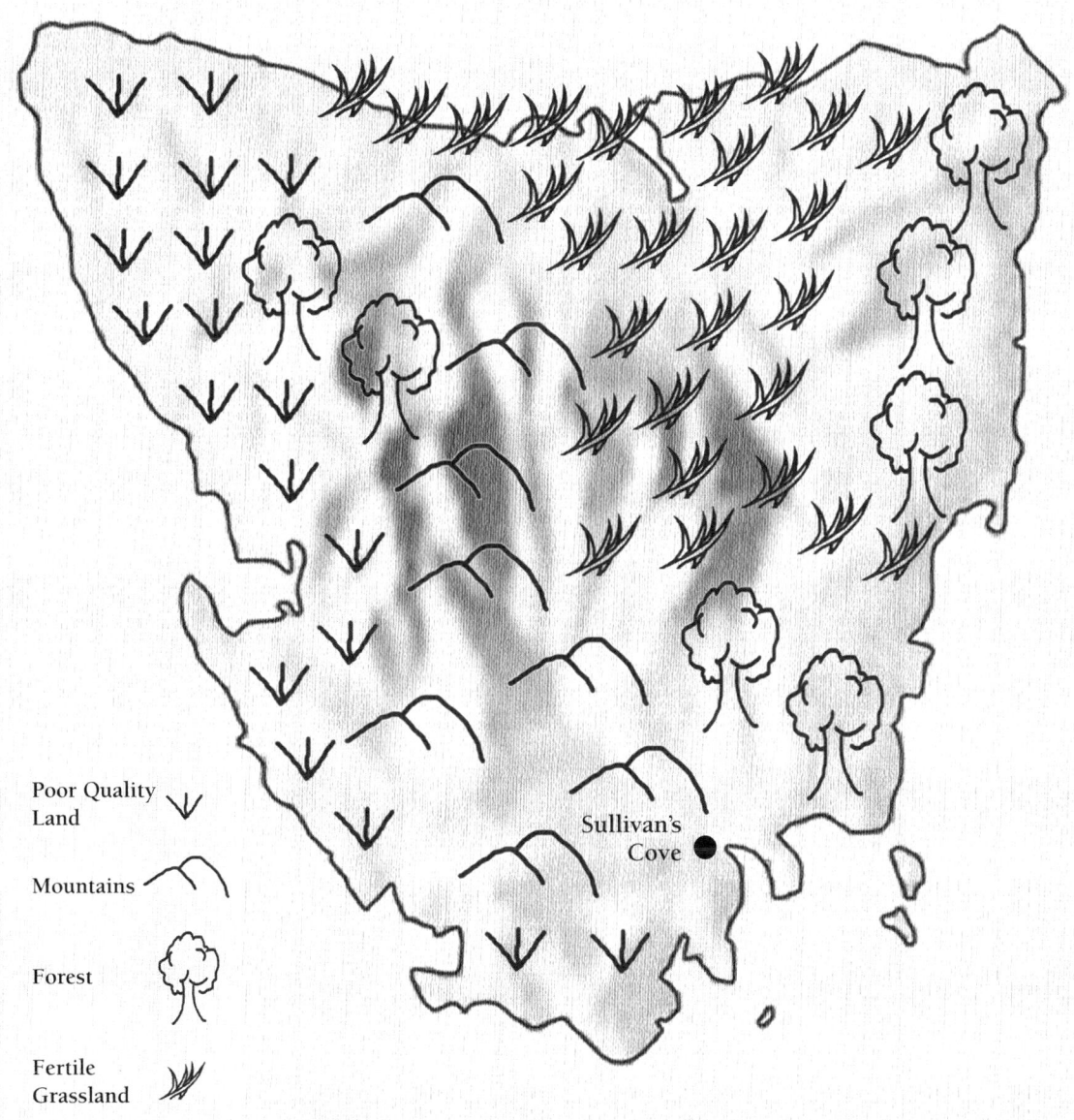

Poor Quality
Land

Mountains

Forest

Fertile
Grassland

Sullivan's
Cove

Two communities live on the island. The Islanders have been there a very long time. The Settlers arrived a year ago.

THE ISLANDERS

You and your ancestors have lived on the Island for a long time. You have never been to any other part of the world. Everything you need is on the Island.

There are about 4,000 Islanders. The Island is large: there is enough space for everyone.

You live in small groups of about 20 people. There are no towns or villages.

Islanders are always on the move. You spend winter near the coast and move to the high land in summer.

As you do not stay in one place for long, you do not plant crops in fields. Your food comes from plants, insects and animals you have hunted. You do not eat fish. You do not like them.

Islanders have no money and very few possessions. The only things you own are your weapons and eating utensils. Everything else you need is shared with the others in your group. When someone kills an animal, the meat is offered to everyone in the group.

There are many special places on the Island, where you believe the spirits of your ancestors live. Every year you must visit these sites to pray to the spirits.

You carry spears and knives. Islanders do not have guns.

THE SETTLERS

You have reached the Island after a long journey by sea. You have come to the Island in search of a better life.

There are now about 1,000 Settlers on the Island.

You live with your family in Sullivan's Cove. This is a small town in the south east of the Island that you and the other Settlers have built.

You are gradually exploring more and more of the Island. As you clear the forest, you plant crops and fence off land in which to keep your sheep and cattle.

You take wood from the forests to build houses and boats. The forests are very large, and you think there will be enough wood to sell to people in other countries. This should be a good way of making you quite a lot of money.

You hunt with guns, rifles and knives.

YOUR COMMUNITY

FOR ISLANDERS AND SETTLERS

1 How long have you lived on the Island?	
2 How many people are there in your community?	
3 What do you eat?	
4 What weapons do you have?	
5 Where do you live?	
6 What use do you make of the environment?	

DECISION CARDS

ISLANDERS 1

Your group is very hungry. After a long search for food you find some sheep grazing. You climb over a fence, kill one of the animals, cut it up and take the meat back to your group.

ISLANDERS 2

Some of the Islanders have been shot at by Settlers trying to scare them away from good grazing land.

ISLANDERS 3

You chase and kill a wild animal. It's shared out and eaten by members of your group.

ISLANDERS 4

When the weather gets hot your group always walks up to the mountains. This year your path is blocked. The land is fenced off and you can't get through. You climb over the fences in order to reach the mountains.

ISLANDERS 5

A Settler meets an Islander woman. They fall in love and live together in a house in the town.

ISLANDERS 6

Settlers start to cut down a large number of trees to start building a second town. This is close to an area where you believe the spirits of your ancestors live.

SETTLERS 1

A number of Islanders come on to your land and kill one of your sheep which was in a fenced-off pasture.

SETTLERS 2

Some Settlers have been shooting at Islanders who came onto land where the Settlers' herds of cattle are grazing.

SETTLERS 3

You see a group of Islanders carrying a dead wild animal they have just killed.

SETTLERS 4

During the summer you spend a lot of time and money building fences to keep in your animals and protect them from attack. The Islanders are climbing over these fences and walking across your land.

SETTLERS 5

A Settler meets an Islander woman. They fall in love and live together in a house in the town.

SETTLERS 6

You find a very good place for building a new town and begin to cut down the forest for wood. Islanders are objecting because this is near one of their sacred sites.

DECISION CARDS - ANSWERS

1   **Islanders kill animals in a fenced area.**

The Settlers' law does not allow people to go on private property. Nor does it let them kill an animal which belongs to someone else. The Islanders would not understand that people could own animals nor why they would want to put a fence around their land.

2   **Settlers shoot at Islanders.**

The grazing land where the shooting has taken place is not fenced off. The Settlers are using force to keep it for themselves.

3   **Islanders kill a wild animal.**

Neither community should object to this.

4   **Islanders cross fences to go to the mountains.**

This would be thought of by the Settlers as trespassing. The Settlers would not know of the summer journey to the mountains and may think of it as trespassing in order to kill cattle or steal crops.

5   **An Islander and a Settler live together.**

The rules and laws of neither community forbid this but with feelings against the other group being so strong, it is likely that this couple would face difficulties from both communities.

6   **Settlers cut down the forest to build a second town.**

The Islanders would not be pleased about this. They would not want parts of the forest to be cut down. In doing this the Settlers may also be destroying some of the Islanders' sacred places which, they believe, contain the spirits of their ancestors.

VAN DIEMAN'S LAND
THE SETTLERS

The island that you have been studying is based on the real island of Tasmania, situated off the south east coast of Australia.

The island was first inhabited by the Aboriginal people when it was still joined to Australia about 40,000 years ago. After the last Ice Age, about 20,000 years ago, the level of the sea rose and Tasmania became an island.

It is thought that Europeans first reached the island in 1629 when survivors came ashore after a ship's mutiny. In 1642 it was visited by a Dutch sailor called Abel Tasman who named the island Van Diemen's Land, after the man who had raised the money for his voyage.

Over the next 100 years, Van Diemen's Land was explored by the French and the British. In 1803 the first British settlement was built at Sullivan's Cove, for a group of 24 convicts who had been sentenced to transportation from England. At this time it was common for criminals to be punished by being sent - or transported, as it was called - to Australia.

Ordinary settlers also came to Van Diemen's Land to farm and fish, hoping for a better life than in their old country.

For the first few months there was little trouble between the Aborigines and the white settlers. But soon problems began to appear, caused by the differences in the two groups' way of life. For example, in 1804 a group of Aborigines were shot as they ran on to a settler's farm while trying to corner a wild kangaroo.

Australia

Tasmania

New Zealand

THE PROBLEM

The Aborigines said ...

THEIR FENCES STOP US MOVING AROUND AS WE HAVE ALWAYS DONE.

IN OUR COUNTRY NO ONE OWNS THINGS. THEY ARE HERE TO BE LOOKED AFTER AND TO BE PASSED ON, NOT TO BE KEPT FOR OURSELVES.

THE SETTLERS HAVE TAKEN OUR LAND.

THEY DESTROY OUR SACRED PLACES.

The Settlers said ...

YOU HAVE TO PUT A FENCE AROUND THE LAND TO STOP THE ANIMALS ESCAPING AND TO KEEP THEM SAFE.

THE ABORIGINES DO NOT NEED ALL THE LAND THEY TRAVEL OVER.

THE ABORIGINES COME ONTO OUR LAND AND KILL OUR ANIMALS. THEY ARE NOT CIVILIZED. THEY DO NOT EVEN WEAR CLOTHES.

Both sides disagree. What do you think happened to these two communities?

THE WAR GOES ON

As more settlers arrived in Van Diemen's Land, the fighting between the British and the Aborigines grew worse. There was violence on both sides but the settlers' weapons made the struggle one-sided. Many Aborigines were shot but many also died from diseases which they caught from the settlers. Some settlers called for their extermination. Sugar and flour laced with poison were left for the Aborigines in special huts. This was against the law, but few white people were punished for harming Aborigines. One reason for this was that Aborigines were not allowed to give evidence in court against their attackers because their religion meant they were unable to swear on the Bible to tell the whole truth.

In 1824 the Governor of the island tried to do something about the killing. He made a law which stated that Aborigines should move to the north-eastern corner of the island where they would be free to lead their own way of life. When they took no notice he tried to have them rounded up like cattle. Still this didn't work.

The Aboriginal people continued to suffer badly and so in 1828 the Governor tried a different approach. He hired a man called George Robinson to go round the island visiting all the remaining Aborigines to persuade them that it would be in their best interests to leave Tasmania and settle on Flinders Island just to the north. It took Robinson and his party five years to reach everyone. By then many had died and in the end only 135 Aborigines finally left for Flinders Island.

Separated from home, the Aborigines were very homesick and more and more died. Eventually, the survivors were brought back to Tasmania but they continued to die of disease and drink. In 1865, the last Tasmanian Aboriginal man died and in 1876 the last surviving woman died. In just over 70 years, the whole Aboriginal population of Tasmania had been wiped out.

In 1828, the Governor of Van Dieman's Land had this poster made for the Aborigines. He wanted to tell them that if a black or white person broke the law, they would be treated the same way.

THE ABORIGINAL PEOPLE TODAY

Topics 1 and 2 of this unit have mainly been about the time when white settlers went to Tasmania to make a living. We have seen that they did not understand Aboriginal beliefs nor the way of life that the Aboriginal people had followed for thousands of years.

The Aboriginal people were also treated badly in other parts of Australia. Some were not allowed to speak their own language. Others lost their lives and their land.

Although life for many Aboriginal people is better than it was 100 years ago, they still suffer a lot of discrimination.

Many live on the edge of towns in very poor housing. Pay and standards of living for Aborigines are still well below those of the white population. Aborigines also suffer worse conditions of education, health and justice. For example, since 1980, there have been over 100 deaths of Aboriginal men whilst being held by the police, generally on minor charges such as being drunk.

One of the biggest problems is with mining. Much of Australia's mineral wealth is found in parts of the country which Aboriginal people believe are sacred. They believe the big holes in the ground destroy the land, 'like our mother with a big cut in her body'.

However, people's understanding of human rights is increasing and the idea is slowly gaining ground that the black people of Australia should have equal rights with white Australians. In 1987, the High Court of Western Australia stopped the Electricity Board from laying a pipeline across an Aboriginal sacred site. This would not have happened 50 years before. Australia now has a Human Rights Commission to promote equal rights for all Australians irrespective of their race, colour or nationality.

THE UNIVERSAL DECLARATION OF HUMAN RIGHTS

In 1948 many countries signed a document called the **Universal Declaration of Human Rights**. This is a list of basic rights which it is thought all people everywhere should have.

Parts of this document are set out below in a simplified form.

The foundation of freedom, justice and peace in the world is the recognition of the dignity and the equal rights of all members of the human family.

All human beings are born free and equal in dignity and rights.

No one should be a slave or be made to work for another person for little reward.

No one should suffer cruel, inhuman or degrading treatment.

Everyone is entitled to the equal protection of the law.

No one should have their property taken away unfairly.

Everyone has the right to freedom of opinion and expression.

Everyone has the right to equal pay for equal work.

Everyone is entitled to the rights above regardless of their race, colour, sex, language, religion, political opinions, nationality, social background, wealth, birth or anything else.

How does the treatment of the Aboriginal people compare with the rights set out in the Universal Declaration of Human Rights?

Trucanini, the last of the Tasmanian Aboriginal people.

After her death in 1876, her skeleton was stored in an apple crate, and then later put on show in an Australian museum. In 1947 it was taken down and again put into store. One hundred years after her death, Trucanini's body was finally cremated and her ashes scattered in the sea.

IS IT THEFT?

A LITTLE EXTRA

Every month John puts a small part of his wages into his account at the local building society. It's not a lot, but it is the only way he can save enough for a holiday with his children.

Each month the building society sends John a statement telling him how much he has in his account. This month John sees that he has much more money than he thought. There must be a mistake. He writes to the building society to say it has given him £20,000 more than it should have.

'No,' says the building society, 'there has been no mistake. The money is yours.'

John writes again. 'We have double checked,' says the building society, 'we have not made a mistake.'

John still isn't happy. He writes for a third time, and the building society tells him again that the money is his.

After this, John doesn't think he has anything to lose. He starts to spend the money on things he and his family need. He buys some new furniture, redecorates his house and goes away on a week's holiday with his family.

A little later, the people at the building society realise that they have made a mistake. The £20,000 that John has been given belongs to another customer of the same name. The building society asks John for the money back. He gives them what he has left, but he has spent more than £10,000. John is charged with theft.

IN COURT

THEFT

If John is to be found guilty of theft, it must be proved in court that he:

● behaved dishonestly, and that he
● took or kept something belonging to someone else, and that he
● intended to keep it permanently.

Should John be found guilty of theft?

To answer this, you need to ask three questions:

1   Did John behave dishonestly?

2   Did John take or keep something belonging to someone else?

3   Did John intend to keep it?

If your answer to all three questions is 'yes', then John is guilty in law.
If you have answered 'no' to one or more then he is not guilty.

If you decide that John is guilty in law of theft, what punishment do you think he should be given?

For a crime of this kind a judge can send a person to prison for up to 10 years or make them pay a fine of up to £2,000.

If you decide that John is not guilty, would you make him pay back to the building society the money that he spent on his family and his home? This was more than £10,000.

OWNING UP

Michael and Rosie are at school. Carl and Lucy, their parents, both work.

Read about the four situations that they have recently found themselves in. Look at each one, and decide whether the law of theft has been broken.

Remember a person has committed theft if she or he:

● has behaved dishonestly and
● takes something belonging to someone else and
● intends to keep it permanently.

Use the table below to set out your answers.

		Your Verdict	Your Reasons
	Someone picks up **Rosie**'s £5.00.		
	Michael is given too much change.		
	Lucy decides to keep the screwdrivers she finds in the back of her car.		
	Carl takes pens and paper from the office.		

Rosie took £5.00 to school. She thinks she dropped the money in the corridor, between maths and French at the start of the last lesson of the day. After school Rosie asks every teacher she can find. Nobody has handed the money in - someone has found and kept it.

Michael's lunch costs £1.85. He pays for it with a £5 note. It's very busy. The dinner lady hands Michael £4.15 in change. Michael says nothing and keeps the money.

A week ago the family car was repaired. As she takes her bag out of the car after work, Lucy notices a set of screwdrivers in the boot. They don't belong to anyone at home. Lucy thinks they were probably left by the mechanic from the garage. No one from the garage has been in touch, so Lucy decides to keep them.

Carl works in an office. He sometimes needs to work at home and so he takes home paper, pens and other stationery which are used by both Carl and the other members of his family.

RIGHT OR WRONG?

ROSIE'S £5.00

The law states that it is an offence to keep something you find, unless you believe that it is not really possible for you to discover who the owner is. If Rosie had lost 10 pence in the corridor between maths and French, anyone finding it would probably think that it would be impossible to find the owner - the money could belong to anyone.

   If the finder of Rosie's money thought the owner could not be found and kept the money, then probably no crime was committed. But if the person who found the money believed that the owner could be found, and still kept quiet, then he or she would have broken the law.

Do you think the person who found Rosie's money, and kept it, broke the law?

MICHAEL'S LUNCH

Michael almost certainly realised that the dinner lady had made a mistake and had given him too much change. If you obtain property by another person's mistake, you have a legal duty to return the property to the owner. By realising that a mistake had been made and not doing anything about it, Michael committed the crime of theft.

What do you think you would have done in Michael's place?

THE SCREWDRIVERS FOUND BY LUCY

Lucy has stolen the screwdrivers from the garage. She knew they did not belong to anyone in her family, but were left there by the mechanic who mended the car. She was being dishonest, and so at the moment she decided to keep the screwdrivers, the theft took place.

Do you think Lucy was wrong to keep the screwdrivers?

CARL'S OFFICE STATIONERY

Carl is guilty of theft. He was not dishonest when he took the pens and paper to use for his work at home. But when he decided that his family could help themselves, he committed the crime of theft.

What would you do about this if you were Carl's boss?

A NICE LITTLE EARNER

1   Ella and Tom, both 13, see a card in the local newsagent's window asking for two young people to do a paper round.

2   They get the job and do well. Soon they are doing extra work for the owner, Mr Wakefield, like unpacking boxes and stacking shelves.

3   Tom and Ella begin to help themselves to goods from the shop. They take them out in the newspaper bags.

4   They tell their friends how easy it is, and take orders for Christmas. The news spreads round the school.

5   A teacher overhears two pupils planning what to ask Tom to take from Mr Wakefield's shop.

WHAT HAPPENS NEXT?

The teacher finds out that 13 pupils have bought things that Tom and Ella have taken from the shop. The teacher tells the head of the school what she has discovered.

Has the law been broken? If so, by whom?

What would you do now if you were the head teacher?

Tom and Ella have broken the law. Do you think they should be reported to the police? Why?

WHAT THE LAW SAYS

It is against the law to take something dishonestly from a shop, which you do not intend to return.

It is against the law to receive or buy things that are stolen if you think they might have been stolen.

It is against the law to ask someone to steal something for you. This is the same as stealing it yourself.

Anyone over the age of 10 can be found guilty of a crime.

REACTIONS

The news is out. Everyone knows what Ella and Tom have been doing. Decide what each person might be thinking and write it in the space underneath their name.

Tom and Ella

They took things from Mr Wakefield's shop, and either kept them for themselves, or sold them to friends.

Mr Wakefield, the shopkeeper

He trusted Tom and Ella and did not realise they were taking things from his shop.

Tom and Ella's friends

They bought many of the things that Tom and Ella had taken.

Tom's and Ella's parents

They knew their children were working for Mr Wakefield, but did not know they were taking things from his shop.

What do you think should happen to Tom and Ella?
Give reasons for your answer.

A NOT SO NICE LITTLE EARNER

SO WHAT DID HAPPEN? ...

The head teacher rang Ella's and Tom's parents and explained that it was thought that their children had been stealing from Mr Wakefield's shop. Their parents agreed to come into school that afternoon.

The head teacher called Ella and Tom to his office and, with their parents there, asked them if they had been stealing and selling items from Mr Wakefield's shop.

Ella and Tom owned up. That evening they went to Mr Wakefield's shop, with their parents, to tell him what they had been doing. They said they were very sorry and promised not to do anything like this again. They promised to pay for everything they had taken and to give back all the stolen goods they could.

Mr Wakefield said that he was prepared to give Ella and Tom a second chance, and would let them continue to work at his shop for a trial period of three months. He did not tell the police.

Ella and Tom handed back the money they had got from their friends, and the goods were returned to the head teacher. Mr Wakefield said that he didn't want the things back since they were now soiled. They were sold at the school's Christmas Bazaar which was being held in a week's time.

◆ Why do you think Mr Wakefield kept Tom and Ella on at the shop?

◆ Do you agree with what happened to them?

◆ What would you have done in Mr Wakefield's position?

◆ Should the young people who bought goods from Tom and Ella have been punished?

◆ Should their parents be told?

In pairs, or groups, make a list of all the reasons you can think of as to why it is wrong to steal. Are some of the reasons better than others? Then compile a class list.

Investigate the extent of theft in your school or in your local area. Local shopkeepers and police officers will have information about what can be done about it.

YOUNG PEOPLE AND CRIME

How Criminal?

Look at the crime figures shown in the two graphs on this page. What do they tell you about recorded crime? Are young people more criminal than adults? In fact, it is very difficult to tell.

Number of males cautioned or found guilty of serious offences for every 100,000 people 1985-1995

Source: Criminal Statistics 1995. HMSO

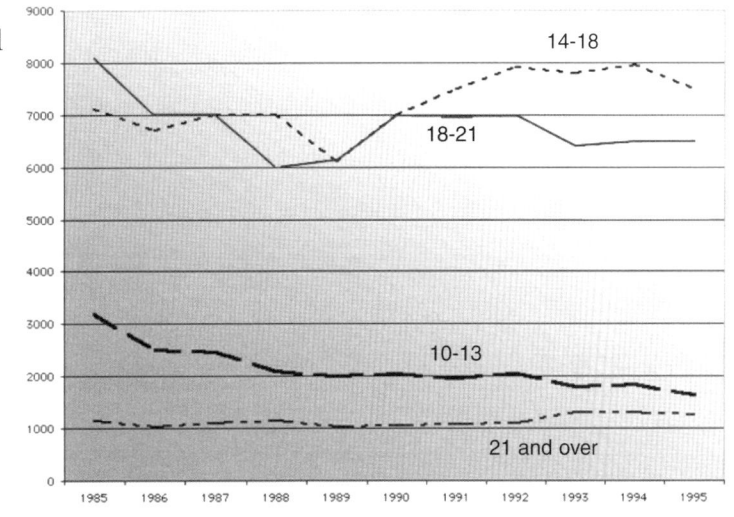

Offenders as a percentage of the population, by gender and age, 1997-98

Source: Home Office

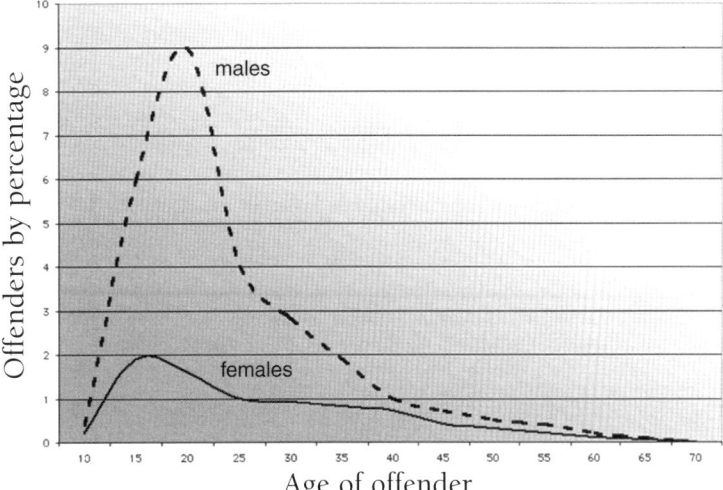

None of this excuses juvenile crime but it can help us to understand why young people may often be looked on by the police with some suspicion. Crime figures can be misleading.

YOUNG PEOPLE MISBEHAVING

Here are some reasons why juvenile crime rates appear to be high:

a)   Young people are high
spirited and spend a lot
of their time out and
about. They are more
likely to be spotted
doing something
wrong by the police.

b)   Young people often
commit offences which
are easy to detect, like
riding vehicles which are
not roadworthy or certain
public order offences.

**Much of the misbehaviour of young
people tends to be in public.**

c)   Young people take more risks and have less to lose than adults.
Certain crimes are committed mostly for adventure. When boys start
going out with girls they tend to settle down.

d)   Most of the offences committed by young people are not of a serious
kind compared with many adult offences.

Discuss which crimes most badly affect young people as victims.
Why is this?

◆   How far do you agree with d) above?

◆   What type of crime do you consider to be the most serious? Why is this?
Is there agreement in the class?

◆   Violent crime appears to be on the increase. Why do you think this
might be? What do you think might be done about this?

◆   Can you add any more reasons to this list of why young people may
become involved in crime?

◆   Is juvenile crime a serious problem? Think of the people affected by it
and how it affects the quality of life.

THE CASE OF LOUISE JONES

1. It's Christmas Eve in a crowded shopping precinct. Several stores have reported thefts. The manager at Kendalls has reported that a young woman, aged about 16, has left the shop and is thought to be carrying stolen goods. The security guards are warned. PC Elaine Fisher also happens to be in the precinct.

...THE GIRL IS OF MEDIUM BUILD WITH LIGHT BROWN HAIR AND IS CARRYING A DISTINCTIVE RED AND YELLOW STRIPED BAG...

2. PC Fisher spots a girl who answers to the description. She has reasonable grounds to suspect that she may have stolen items in her bag. She stops the girl and asks her what is in her bag. She has to explain why she wants to do this.

3. The girl says her name is Louise Jones. In her bag, Louise has a bottle of expensive perfume, and some blank cassettes. She says that she bought them all in the same shop but has lost the receipt. Louise has no money on her.

4. Louise is arrested and cautioned* by PC Fisher. She is taken to the police station. If she was not under arrest, she would not have to go with the officer.

5. The police phone Louise's parents straight away. If her parents cannot get to the station, the police will try to contact another adult, like a social worker, to be with Louise during the interview.

6. When Louise's parents arrive, she is told of her legal rights. Louise has the right to free legal advice from a solicitor.

7. During the interview, Louise admits taking the goods. The whole of the interview is recorded.

8. After Louise has been charged with theft she is released on bail. The police later recommend to the Crown Prosecution Service that Louise should be charged.

9. A few weeks later, Louise appears in the Youth Court** and is represented by the solicitor who is paid through the legal aid system. Louise pleads guilty to the charges. The magistrates are then told that Louise has been in trouble before.

10. The magistrates ask for a report on Louise's circumstances before they decide what sentence to pass. So someone from the Youth Offending Team visits the family to prepare a report for the court. The magistrates need this information to decide what will be best for Louise.

Note

* In the caution, Louise is told that she does not have to say anything but, if she doesn't, this could count against her if she later mentions something in court that she failed to mention at the time of her arrest.

* The Youth Court deals with offenders between 10 and 17, unless the offence is very serious.

WHICH SENTENCE?

Look at the sentences below. Which do you think is the most suitable for Louise?

Louise has twice been in trouble with the police for shoplifting. She has received a final warning. She admits to a drug habit.

Reprimand

A telling off by a senior police officer, given to first time offenders for offences which are not serious.

Final warning

When someone is given a final warning, their case is looked at by the Youth Offending Team, who work with the young person to try to change their behaviour.

Conditional discharge

No sentence is passed on a first offence but the court places some conditions on the offender. If they break these conditions, they will come back to court on the original charge.

Referral Order

First time offenders can be referred to a Youth Offender Panel. The panel will agree a contract with the offender and his or her family, aimed at tackling the offending behaviour. It could include paying something back to the victim, an apology, family counselling or drug rehabilitation.

Action Plan Order

These last for three months. They are designed to help the offender improve their behaviour and can include meeting and apologising to the victim.

Reparation Order

Reparation means 'making up for what you have done'. It can include meeting the victim, apologising or paying something back. It might mean that criminal damage has to be repaired.

Supervision Order

This can last up to three years. The person must report regularly to a member of the Youth Offending Team and can be made to do certain activities like attending a drugs education course. They can also be made to 'make up' for their behaviour in some way (reparation).

Community Service

This is unpaid work in the community for a certain number of hours.

(Young people committing serious violent or sexual offences can be locked up in secure centres from the age of 12. So can persistent young offenders but this will not apply in Louise's case.)

WHAT THE LAW SAYS

POLICE POWERS

Stop and search

1   Police officers may stop and search anyone in a public place whom they reasonably suspect is carrying stolen or 'prohibited goods' like drugs or weapons.

2   Before a search is carried out, the police officers must give their names, the police station they are from and the reason for the search. The officers should make a written record of the search when it has taken place. A copy of this can be asked for anytime over the next 12 months.

Arrest

3   The police can arrest anyone they reasonably suspect has committed or is about to commit certain offences ('arrestable offences'). They include theft, assault, drug offences, vandalism and some public order offences.

4   The police must explain why the arrest has been made and tell the person that they have the right to remain silent, but that this could count against them if they fail to mention anything which they later bring up in court. Anyone who is not under arrest does not have to go to the police station. A person can be arrested for giving a false name and address.

WHAT THE LAW SAYS CONTINUED...

In the police station

5   A person who is not under arrest can leave the police station whenever he or she wishes. If the police do not want this to happen, then that person must be arrested.

6   People arrested by the police have the right to see a solicitor and have someone else told of their arrest. These rights can be refused for 36 hours if the offence is very serious and the police feel this would seriously affect their enquiries.

     Someone suspected of terrorism can be denied legal advice for up to 48 hours.

In detention

7   Police can normally hold suspects at the station for up to 24 hours. This can be extended by a senior officer to 36 hours. The maximum anyone can be held for questioning without being charged is 96 hours (but only with the permission of a magistrate). This does not apply to suspects on terrorist charges.

Confession

8   The Police and Criminal Evidence Act 1984 lays down that statements admitting guilt must not be obtained by 'oppression'. This includes, 'torture, inhuman or degrading treatment, and the use or threat of violence'.

     Suspects must be allowed eight hours' continuous rest in any 24-hour period. They must be provided with at least two light meals and one main meal with refreshment breaks every two hours.

◆   Why do you think all these rules are so strictly laid down?

◆   Do you think any of these rules should be changed? If so, why?

◆   Why can the police not use threats and other methods to get criminals to admit their guilt?

OUT OF THE BLUE

SOLDIERS GUARD THE STREETS
POLICE ON STRIKE - EXTENSIVE LOOTING

From Our Special Correspondent, 4th August 1919

CENTRAL Liverpool tonight represents a war zone, and as I write this evening the report comes that there have been firing and woundings. Army lorries and tanks, carrying large numbers of men, stand by waiting for any call that might be made.

Shops along London Road and elsewhere are boarded up, but in most cases this has come too late, for last night boot shops, jewellers and furniture stores were smashed, looted and wrecked.

The trouble began late on Friday night with an attack on the shop of Mr Latarche, a jeweller in London Road, where looters, after smashing the window, got away with valuables.

Gangs of youths and men walked down the street stopping at one shop, then another. The air sounded with the crash of huge plate glass windows as youths jumped into the shops and made a grab for the things inside.

In one district, women talked with the men, telling them which shops to steal from.

A CASUALTY

Looters forced their way into the bottling factory of J.P. O'Brien and Co., and helped themselves to all kinds of liquor. What they could not drink they took away in handcarts. Soldiers arrived and caught the looters red-handed. The soldiers were stoned and mobbed by the crowd, and at last warning shots were fired. As a result, Thomas Howlett of Skirving Street fell badly wounded. He is in the Northern Hospital in a critical condition with a bullet in his thigh.

THE POLICE ARE ON STRIKE

Pay in the police had always been low, and in 1918, many officers were paid so little that they and their families did not have enough money for food.

Some officers set up a trade union to try to get better wages for the police, but the government was against this, and so, in August 1918, most of the police in London went on strike.

Although 12,000 police officers stopped work, there was very little crime and the strike soon ended when the government offered the police more money.

But the government would not recognise the police trade union, and it was because of this that the second strike was called. Most police officers, however did not want to strike, and it was only in Liverpool that a large number of officers stopped work.

◆ Who do you think was to blame for the riots in Liverpool? Was it the government, the police, or the rioters?

◆ Do you think the government was right not to allow police officers to form a trade union? What are the problems of allowing people who serve the public to go on strike? What are the problems with banning public servants from striking?

◆ If the police went on strike today, how do you think it would affect you and the community in which you live?

CONSEQUENCES	
For me and my family	For the community where I live

When the police went on strike, members of the public were asked to sign on as 'special constables'. Would you have been willing to do this?

NEW RECRUITS

POLICE DUTIES

On patrol	33%
Traffic incidents	5%
Dealing with crimes	10%
Call out	5%
Attending court	14%
Station duties	8%
Report writing	16%
Meals and refreshment	9%

POLICE OFFICERS

Total no. of officers	126,000
Female	21,000
Male	105,000
Officers from ethnic minorities	2,700
Records taken	31.3.2000

Imagine your local police force is going to appoint TEN new police officers.

◆ What sort of person would make a good police officer in the area where you live?

◆ Describe the qualities that you would look for.

◆ How many of the officers should be women?

◆ How many of the officers should come from ethnic minority groups?

ACTION STATIONS

LOCAL RESIDENTS ARE FURIOUS

IT'S TERRIBLE AROUND HERE. NOTHING IS SAFE. EVERY DAY SOMEONE IN THIS AREA HAS THEIR HOME BROKEN INTO.

THERE ARE LIGHTS ON HERE ALL NIGHT. OLD PEOPLE ARE AFRAID TO GO TO SLEEP IN CASE THEY ARE BURGLED. ONE LADY IS SO SCARED SHE KEEPS A TRUNCHEON WITH HER ALL THE TIME.

LAST NIGHT THEY STOLE A CAR. IT BELONGS TO A MAN WHO TAKES HIS WIFE TO HOSPITAL EVERY DAY FOR KIDNEY TREATMENT.

SOMETHING MUST BE DONE

WHAT NEXT?

People in this community are angry about all these thefts. You are one of a group of residents who want to do something about the problem.

On your own, make a note of all the things that you can think of which could be done to make the community safer.

Share these with the other members of your group, and draw up an action plan of what you, as a group, think should be done.

TAKING THE LAW INTO THEIR OWN HANDS

Here are two ways in which people have tried to beat the problem of crime in their community.

VIGILANTES PATROL STREETS

VIGILANTE PATROLS have taken to the streets of Milton Yardley to 'control crime'. Military-style units have vowed to 'clear the streets' in response to recent attacks on local residents, particularly children. Two patrols were on the streets last weekend, carrying walkie-talkies and accompanied by a rottweiler and a doberman.

The anti-crime patrols say they will question anyone they regard as acting suspiciously. A spokesman said, "We are taking the law into our own hands. If the cops can't protect our kids, then we will."

When asked if the units would resort to violence, he replied, "I cannot say how our people will react if faced with an attacker."

STAMPING OUT CRIME

GANGS OF TEENAGERS have been roaming around Grimthorpe's Rivers Estate trying the doors on almost every home and car in the street. Now, from dusk to dawn every night, groups of men patrol the estate. Anyone acting suspiciously is watched and reported to the police.

More than 80 people, aged from 17 to 66, have joined the scheme. Their powerful torches and blue anoraks have been bought with money given by residents. Two housewives organise the group's rota and ring the police every third night to provide a list of patrolmen on duty.

A list of local residents who have agreed to their telephones being used to call the police has been drawn up.

Mr Carl Roberts, who started the residents' groups, says, "We don't go out looking for trouble, but things are so bad, we have to help ourselves."

VIGILANTES PATROL STREETS

VIGILANTE PATROLS have taken to the streets of Milton Yardley to 'control crime'. Military-style units have vowed to 'clear the streets' in response to recent attacks on local residents, particularly children. Two patrols were on the streets last weekend, carrying walkie-talkies and accompanied by a rottweiler and a doberman.

The anti-crime patrols say they will question anyone they regard as acting suspiciously. A spokesman said, "We are taking the law into our own hands. If the cops can't protect our kids, then we will."

When asked if the units would resort to violence, he replied, "I cannot say how our people will react if faced with an attacker."

STAMPING OUT CRIME

GANGS OF TEENAGERS have been roaming around Grimthorpe's Rivers Estate trying the doors on almost every home and car in the street. Now, from dusk to dawn every night, groups of men patrol the estate. Anyone acting suspiciously is watched and reported to the police.

More than 80 people, aged from 17 to 66, have joined the scheme. Their powerful torches and blue anoraks have been bought with money given by residents. Two housewives organise the group's rota and ring the police every third night to provide a list of patrolmen on duty.

A list of local residents who have agreed to their telephones being used to call the police has been drawn up.

Mr Carl Roberts, who started the residents' groups, says, "We don't go out looking for trouble, but things are so bad, we have to help ourselves."

◆ How do these stories, which are based on fact, compare with your action plan?

◆ What are the differences between the two groups? Would you be in favour of either of these patrols in your area?

◆ How do you think the police would react to these groups?

◆ What are the dangers of people taking the law into their own hands?

◆ Find out about the role of Neighbourhood Watch Schemes in your area.

◆ Find out whether any Youth Action groups are actively combating crime in your area.